An Introduction to
Needle
Felting

An Introduction to
Needle
Felting

Linda Calver

WHITE OWL

AN IMPRINT OF PEN & SWORD BOOKS LTD.
YORKSHIRE - PHILADELPHIA

First published in Great Britain in 2022 by
Pen & Sword WHITE OWL
An imprint of
Pen & Sword Books Ltd
Yorkshire – Philadelphia

ISBN 9781526780645

Printed and bound in the UK, by Short Run Press Limited, Exeter.

Design: Paul Wilkinson

Pen & Sword Books Limited incorporates the imprints of Atlas, Archaeology, Aviation, Discovery, Family History, Fiction, History, Maritime, Military, Military Classics, Politics, Select, Transport, True Crime, Air World, Frontline Publishing, Leo Cooper, Remember When, Seaforth Publishing, The Praetorian Press, Wharncliffe Local History, Wharncliffe Transport, Wharncliffe True Crime and White Owl.

For a complete list of Pen & Sword titles please contact:
PEN & SWORD BOOKS LIMITED
47 Church Street, Barnsley, South Yorkshire, S70 2AS, England
E-mail: enquiries@pen-and-sword.co.uk
Website: www.pen-and-sword.co.uk

Or
PEN AND SWORD BOOKS
1950 Lawrence Rd, Havertown, PA 19083, USA
E-mail: Uspen-and-sword@casematepublishers.com
Website: www.penandswordbooks.com

Contents

Introduction

WELCOME TO MY BOOK! A little bit about me.

I am a self-taught hobby felter and have been needle felting for the last eight years. I like to do occasional craft fairs and I run a variety of workshops teaching mainly needle felting but also some wet felting, which I touch on in Chapter 7.

I love the versatility of working with wool fleece and find the endless ideas of what you can create from it just so exciting! You don't have to be an incredible artist to achieve wonderful things in this craft, although it does take a little patience and practice to get it right. I also must warn you it is highly addictive. Just the sight and smell of piles of beautiful wool fleece is just heavenly. Wool can be purchased pre-dyed in hundreds of beautiful colours and shades, and there are many different natural colours of wool fleece, varying in colour and texture for all the different breeds of sheep they are taken from.

In this book I will teach you the basics, starting off with easy simple shapes and progressing through to slightly more difficult projects, all of which are suitable for you to start learning about the wonderful art of needle felting. I hope you enjoy working through this book as much as I have enjoyed producing it!

The History of Needle Felting

NEEDLE FELTING IS the process of tangling wool fleece using a barbed needle and using this to sculpt it into shapes. This process can allow the crafter to make the wool into 3-dimensional animals, people or all sorts of wonderful creations, by sculpting shapes, attaching them together and adding more wool layers.

Using sheep and other animal fleece to make felt dates back hundreds of years, but the craft of needle felting started around the 1980s and continues to grow in popularity. Prior to that, felt was made industrially with needles, much the same process we use today in our needle felting but on a huge scale with hundreds of needles in large machines to produce felt in sheets from wool fleece.

You can use other animal fleeces in needle felting, such as alpaca, and mohair. Not all of these types of fleece needle felt well, but sometimes they could be useful to use as fur for the coat or on the surface of a project.

Tools and Materials

MAIN TOOLS

Some of the main tools you will need for the projects in this book include:
- Sponge/pad/other felting surface
- Needles
- Needle holder
- Needle container
- Finger guards
- Awl
- Pipe cleaners
- Pliers
- Scissors
- Wire cutters
- Animal eyes or beads
- Wooden skewer and cocktail stick

FELTING SURFACES

Felting surfaces or pads are used to work on to protect your needle from hitting the table underneath, which could snap your needles.

I mainly use a felting pad made of high-density foam of at least 6cm (2in) thick. The size pad I find ideal for most projects is 21cm x 21cm (8in x 8in), which you can purchase online easily. To protect the sponge from the needles and extend the lifetime of the pad, I use a piece of pure wool felt laid over the top of the mat. This is optional, however, and I only use this because I do a LOT of felting! For felting something that is flat we can also use a Clover felting brush which is great for this purpose, especially used in conjunction with the Clover punch tool.

FELTING NEEDLES

Felting needles are long, steel needles that have tiny barbs on the ends. It is the action of these barbs when pushed into the fleece that tangle the fibres and cause the wool to felt together, which with repeated stabbing forms a shape. The needles come in different shapes like triangles, stars, twisted and reverse, all of which are better suited to some jobs than others.

Needles also come in different gauges of thickness to suit various stages of your work, the higher the gauge being finer and lower gauges being coarser. A 42 gauge is very fine, whilst 32 gauge is very coarse, with various gauges in between.

I mainly use 38, 40 and 42 gauges in triangle shape, and very occasionally a 36, so to keep things simple for this book, these are what we will be using for the projects. When using more than one needle I use the pink Clover pen tool which is super and very comfortable to use. This comes already loaded with three medium needles. The green and yellow Clover punch tool is a very handy tool to own as it assists greatly with flat felting and also for smoothing your 3-dimensional figures for a nice finish. All tools are made in such a way that it is easy to replace any broken needles.

Needles are extremely brittle and can break very easily, so while you are beginning your needle felting I would suggest purchasing a few of each size to have at hand! When felting, always insert the needle and pull it back out again in the same direction. Never try to bend the needle when it is inside your work, as this will snap the tip off. There is a stockist list at the back of the book. Please note that most people who sell needles have their own colour code for sizes of needles, so go by the gauge and not the colour when buying replacements. I mention this as it was something that I got confused with when I first started needle felting, and I ordered the same colour from a different seller and of course, they were a different gauge.

Always dispose of any broken needles safely! There may be times when you break a needle with the tip being left inside your project, so you may need to cut it out if you cannot find it. If this should happen, just cover the area you cut open with more wool.

To protect your needles when you are not using them, store in a suitable container. Very often, needles come in a protective plastic tube when you buy them, which you can use to store them in safely.

NEEDLE HANDLE/HOLDER

It is perfectly fine to just hold the needle at the top when you are felting, however, you may find it more comfortable to put the needle into a holder. You can buy holders that hold a single needle and some that hold two, three or more needles for faster felting of a larger item. I mainly use a Clover pen tool, as it is what I find most comfortable. These are readily available both online and from good craft shops. They are very good and comfortable to use, while also being easy to change a needle if you should break one. I have three Clover pens altogether, each loaded with three needles in each of the three gauges I use most (38, 40, and 42). I also have a single needle in each size, which I usually use without a handle; however, I do have a wooden handle to use if I am doing a lot of single needle work. I keep them all together in a mug with an old piece of sponge inside so they are safe while I am not using them. Whilst working you can keep them in your felting surface.

FINGER GUARDS

Finger guards are usually made of leather or rubber, designed to wear on your thumb and index finger. These protect you from being stabbed with the needle when working. I find them a bit cumbersome, but it is up to you on how you feel about getting the occasional stab or two! An accidental stab with the needle will cause you to bleed, and I am afraid does hurt a bit, although it only lasts a few seconds, and the more you do, the less you will stab yourself. The decision is up to you. You could also try popping a plaster on those fingers, which will protect you a little, if you don't want to use finger guards. When needle felting, always concentrate on your hands and don't look up at the TV!

Needles & Pad.

Clover Brush & Punch Tool.

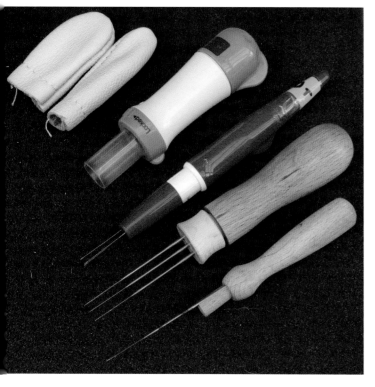

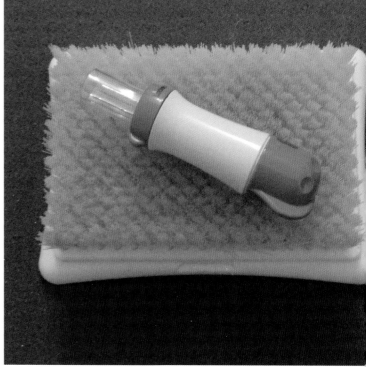

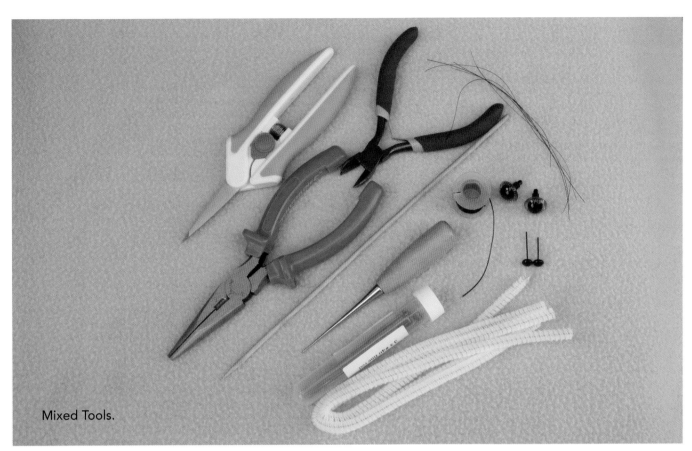

Mixed Tools.

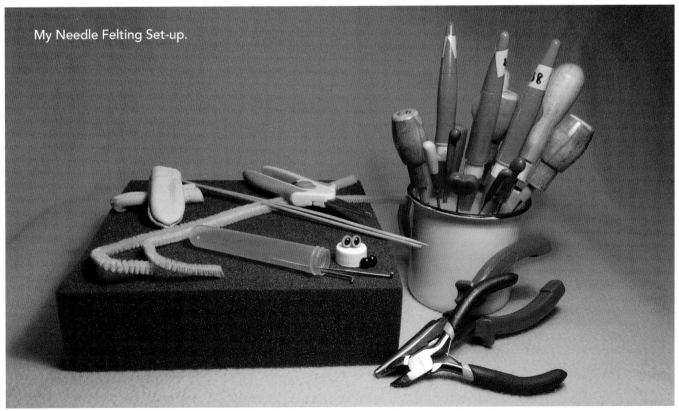

My Needle Felting Set-up.

TOOLS FOR WET FELTING

- Bubble wrap
- Plastic larger than the piece you are felting
- Water sprinkler (you can make one from a plastic milk bottle with holes punched into the lid)
- Warm water
- Sponge
- Old towels
- Any low suds soap (olive oil soap is good)
- Bamboo mat or Pool noodle
- Piece of netting (net curtain is fine)

Wet Felting Tools & Materials.

WOOL FLEECE

There are many different breeds of sheep, and therefore many different fleeces, some of which are more suited to certain types of felting than others. These range from fine wools like merino, which is very soft so ideal for making clothing, scarves, slippers etc., to very coarse wools. The best wools for needle felting are the medium to coarse types. There are also two main methods of washing and preparing fleece for felting and spinning, after which the fleece is either left natural or dyed.

TYPE 1: CARDED WOOL

Carded wool, once processed, has short, springy fibres that lie in different directions, which makes it ideal for needle felting. I always

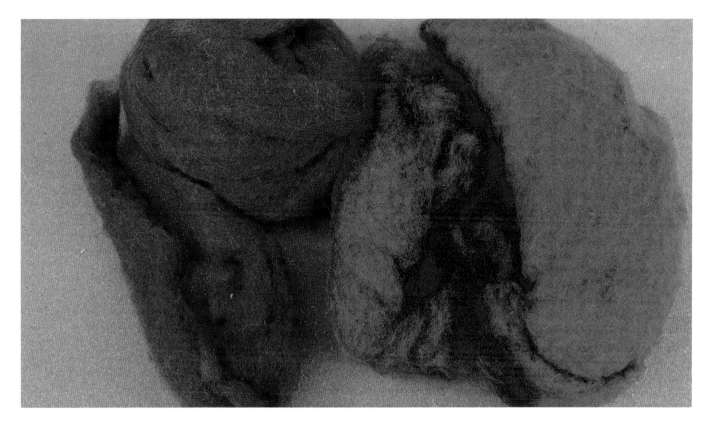

use carded wool for needle felting, and the projects in this book are in the main made using this wool. I mostly use New Zealand, Karacul, Bergschaf, Jacob, Corriedale, Shetland and Merino. You can buy carded wool in a batt form, which is carded wool that comes in a sheet, approximately 52cm (20in) wide, but the size can vary from different suppliers. It also comes in a sliver, which is carded wool in a long strip.

Carded Wool Sliver [left] & Carded Wool Batt [right]

CARDED CORE WOOL

This is carded wool, usually left undyed, which has gone through slightly less of the preparation process and so is a little cheaper to buy. This may contain a little more vegetable matter than other carded wool, due to this less vigorous preparation process. Many needle felters choose to use this as the core of their subjects, and save the other, more expensive, dyed wool for the outer layer. I have used core wool in batt form in most of the projects in the book.

TYPE 2: COMBING (WOOL TOPS)

After the washing process, the wool fleece is combed smooth until all the fibres are running in the same direction, and all the short

Wool Tops.

pieces removed. This leaves the wool very soft and wispy, ideal for wet felting or making anything that will be worn next to the skin, such as a scarf or other clothing. This wool, however, isn't very easy to needle felt with.

TYPE 3: WOOL LOCKS

These are the beautiful curls that have been shorn from the curly coated breeds of sheep, including Wensleydale, Teeswater, Blue-faced Leicester, white Leicester and Lincoln. Wool locks come in a variety of lengths, curls, and crimps depending on the breed of sheep. These can be purchased easily online either raw (unwashed) for you to prepare yourself, or ready washed and either left natural or dyed in a huge array of beautiful colours. Wool locks can be used in needle felting for hair on dolls, bird wings, tails, sheep coats, cats, dogs and much more, or may be used as embellishment and texture on a wet felted bag, purse or picture. There really is no limit to what these can be used for! I usually buy mine ready washed and dyed, although they are more expensive this way.

TYPE 4: WOOL NEPPS

Wool nepps are a by-product of wool processing, and are quite simply just tiny little balls or pieces of wool that are already felted. These are too solid to needle felt with but are great for

embellishment, fixed on to your work using a little piece of carded wool felted in over the top to hold them down, as shown in Chapter 2. You can also use them as embellishment in wet felting.

TIPS AND TRICKS

Tearing off the Batt.

Throughout the book, we will be mainly using a carded batting. To prepare your batting for use, unroll it first and note it may vary in size. To tear off some fleece in a strip, hold one hand flat on the batting and with the other hand gently pull off what you need, either a thin or thick strip.

In most projects at some point, you will be tearing off strips of fleece to an approximate size. Don't worry if it isn't exact or level at the sides; just pull off another small piece and lay it where you need a bit more wool and you can just patch it up until you have the desired size.

When needle felting, it is always better to build your shape up in multiple thin layers, rather than one

Types of Processed Wool: Wool Locks (far left), Wool top (top middle) Wool batt (top right) Wool Sliver (front left) Wool Nepps (front right)

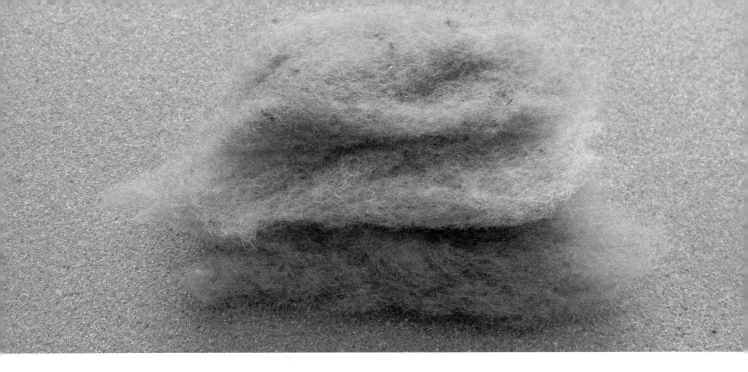

Stack Ready to Hand Blend.

thick one. This is because one thick layer will take longer and be more difficult to felt, and you may not get the core of your shape felted properly as it will be difficult to get the barbs of the needle in deep enough. Therefore, always aim to get the core of your shape firmly felted first, and then make it larger by adding layers, felting as you go.

Sometimes it is a nice touch, particularly on the animals, to mix two or three shades of a colour to get a certain look. To do this, stack a piece of each shade/colour on top of each other, then pick up the stack and, holding each end, pull them apart. Restack the two halves and then repeat the process, continuing to repeat until the colours are nicely blended. If your subject is large, you may have to do this a few times to get enough blended fleece to cover it.

Hand Blending the Stack.

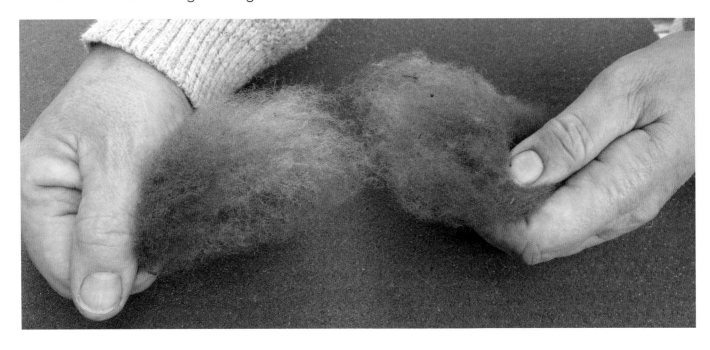

CHAPTER ONE

Simple Shapes

Four mini shapes to get you started. These can be used in lots of ways which you will see later in the book.

FOR ALL THE PROJECTS in this book, I would encourage you to have available a few of all the sizes of needles I mentioned and try them all for yourself as you go along to see how well each needle felts. This will help you learn which to use and when. The lower the gauge number, the thicker and coarser the needle, so I suggest a 36 triangle or 38 triangle needle would be a good choice to start a project with. This depends a little on the breed type of wool you are using, so I encourage you to try them both and you will soon work out which one you are progressing best with; you will feel it working when you have the correct one. The 40 and the 42 gauge triangle needles are finer, and leave a smaller hole in the felt, therefore these are really very useful for smoothing and finishing off your project. As a basic selection to start off with, I would have some of each size to hand, along with a pen tool and if possible, a punch tool, all as described in the tools and equipment chapter.

The speed at which you felt isn't important and I suggest starting slowly until you become more confident, and as with most things, the more you do the easier it will become!

For this Simple Shapes chapter, you will need:

- Carded wool batting in your choice of colour
- 36/38/40/42 triangle single needles (there are other shapes such as Star and twisted but to keep it simple I suggest for you to use triangles which is what I learnt with)
- Clover pen tool (comes loaded with medium needles) or a multi-needle tool with 40 gauge and another one with 42 gauge needles in
- Clover punch tool (optional)
- Wooden skewer

Flower shape.

FLOWER

1. Take your wool batting, which will be in a bundle, and unfold it. Sometimes this can be in layers, which you can split if needed in future, but for this chapter this isn't needed so leave it as it is.

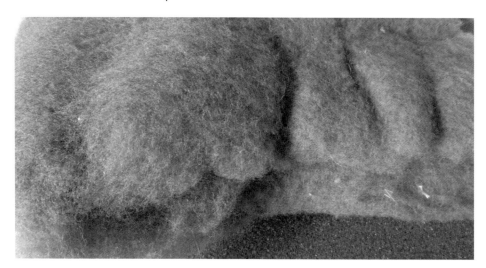

2. To make your petals, from your batting pull off six equal pieces at approximately 8cm (3in) in diameter. Tidy the edges up on each by folding any loose, wispy ends underneath.

3. Take one petal and lay it on your pad, then fold the top half downwards.

4. Holding your petal with one hand and your pen/multi tool in the other, poke your needles in and out of the wool over the whole surface area several times, to start felting your work.

5. Now continue felting until you have the whole petal just lightly felted – be careful not to over-felt the petal so it becomes too solid, as you still need to fold this again at a later stage. Make sure to peel your work up from the pad occasionally, as you don't want to felt your work to your pad! You should now have a semi-circle shape lightly felted.

6. Next, with the straight edge at the top, fold the semi-circle over three times tightly, and felt the edge down straight away to make sure it doesn't unroll.

7. Now you need to felt around three edges to create a nice petal shape, leaving the thinner end of the petal unfelted and wispy, ready for joining all the petals together later. To do this, place your fingers firmly flat on top and start to felt into the three edges to form the petal shape. Then turn the petal over and do the same from the other side. Once you have a nice edge on your petal, felt the petal all over to make it nice and smooth.

8. Repeat steps 2–7 another five times, so you end up with six felted petals of the same size. Don't worry if one petal ends up smaller than the others – you can just add a little more wool by wrapping it round the petal and felting into it to make it slightly bigger.

9. Next lay all six petals together on your pad with the wispy edges into the middle of the flower, to get ready to assemble.

10. Starting with two petals, overlap their loose ends and felt them together. Once these are secure, add the rest of the petals to form your flower.

11. At this point, I like to add a little wool of a different colour to the ends of the petals. To do this, take a small wisp of the different colour wool, lay over the part you wish and simply felt on to secure. This is an optional bit of extra detail if you prefer.

12. Now to add the flower centre! Taking a small piece of wool in any colour, fold it into a circle the right size for the centre of your flower and lay it in the middle of the petals. To fix this to the flower, felt it around the edge into the petals.

13. To finish the flower, you can either felt the centre just a little to let it stand proud from the flower, or you can felt it until it lies flat to the petals if you prefer. Like with the petals, if you decide the centre is too small, you can add a small wisp of wool and felt this on to make it slightly bigger. You could also do this with a different colour to add a little more detail as another option.

Heart shape.

HEART SHAPE

1. Pull a piece of wool off your batting of colour choice, tidying the edges up by folding any thin wispy edges under, and finishing with a piece approximately 10cm x 13cm (5in x 4in).

2. Place this on your pad, fold it in half lengthwise, from the top to the bottom and using a multi needle, felt this down so it is reasonably firm but not too solid to fold. Felting it by poking your needle in diagonally, towards the middle, will prevent the felt from stretching and getting too large.

3. Next fold the two bottom corners into the middle to meet each other, forming a triangle with point at the bottom, then felt these folds down to secure. And now felt the shape all over.

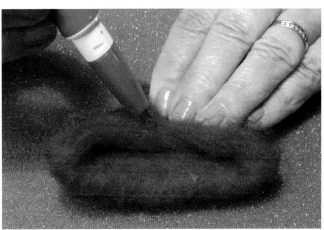

4. Now turn your triangle sideways to you so you can work on the curved top line of the heart. Place your fingers flat on top firmly and in your other hand with a single needle, felt horizontally into the middle of the straight edge of the triangle repeatedly until you form an indentation.

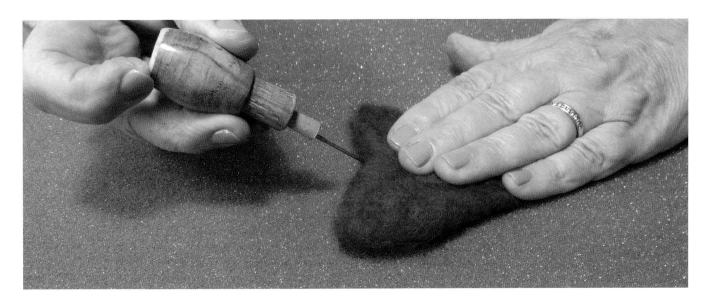

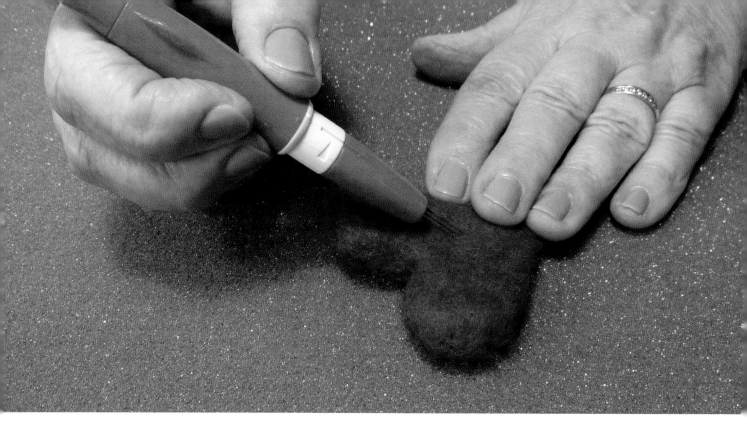

5. Next you need to needle felt around all three edges to perfect the shape, rounding up the edges on the top part of the heart to create the smooth curves and defining the point on the bottom. Remember, the more you felt the smaller it will become.

6. If you need or want to make the heart bigger you can wrap another layer of wool around and felt it on, or if you would like the heart to be thicker, then you can add more wool on the top surface of the heart and felt it down lightly and then add another layer completely over the heart so you don't have any lines where you joined the extra wool on.

7. If you are happy with the size, and haven't added a final layer over, then add a thin layer of wool completely over the whole heart and felt this on to your base heart lightly. This is the time to try out your 40 and 42 gauge needles to finish off the surface of your heart, as these will leave smaller holes giving a smoother finish. If you just use the very ends of the needle where the barbs are when doing this, it will give the smoothest and best finish.

Ball shape

BALL SHAPE

1. From the colour batting of your choice, pull off a long strip approximately 18cm x 8cm (7in x 3in). Lay your wool on your pad lengthwise and fold the length in half.

2. Starting from the end nearest you, tightly roll the wool upwards, folding any loose fibres from the sides in as you go. You may find once you have got going with the rolling it is easier to pick it up from the pad to finish rolling it up, just remember to keep it tight as the tighter it is, the easier it will be to felt.

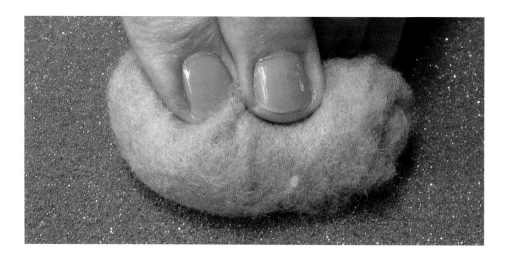

3. Once you have it rolled up, holding it tightly, lay it down on your pad and felt the ends firmly down to secure it, so it doesn't unroll. It will look slightly barrel-shaped at this point.

4. Now you can work on the sides and the loose ends to start forming the ball. Start by felting the ends horizontally inwards, which will help to start forming more of a ball shape. Carry on felting all over the ball, holding it on the pad between your fingers rolling it around as you felt until you have a nice round shape. Sometimes try picking the ball up and rolling it firmly in your hands as this can help get a nice, round shape.

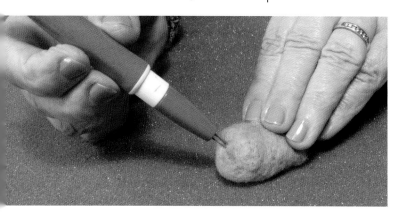

5. Now decide whether you are happy with the size or not. If you are, use a 40 or 42 gauge needle to go over the ball to smooth and finish the work. However, if you want to make it larger for different projects, wrap the ball in another thin layer of wool and felt this layer on. You can keep layering and building this up to the size you desire; however, be sure to do this in multiple thin layers not one thick one. Once you are happy, use the finer needles to finish the project.

TOADSTOOLS

1. Let us start with the stalk. You could use white, off-white, beige or any suitable stalk colour. Pull off a strip of batting, approximately 15cm x 6cm (6in x 2in), and using the pointed end of your wooden skewer, wrap the wool very tightly around it and keep building it up to the desired thickness. You can wind it around or I find it easiest to hold the wool and stick in one hand, and then turn the stick towards

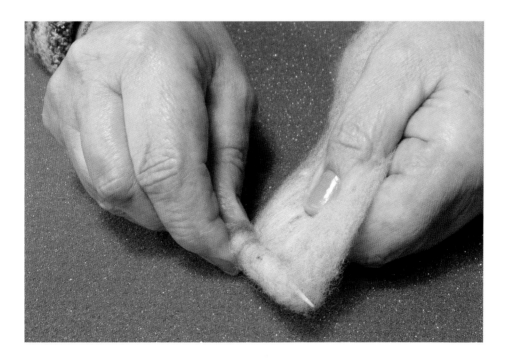

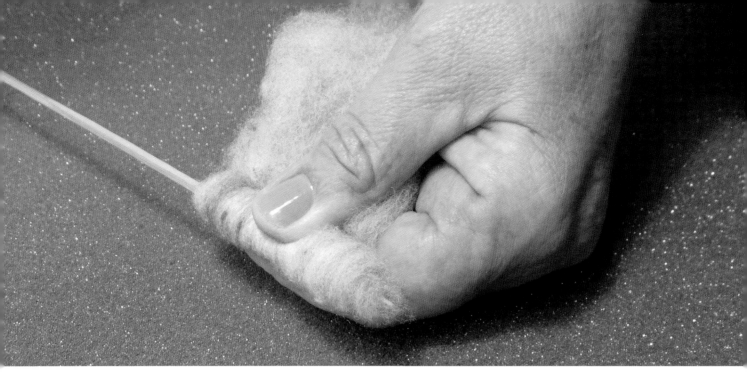

you with the other hand, keeping your thumb firmly on the wool. How far the wool is rolled down the skewer is how long your stalk will be so you need to judge this so it doesn't travel down too far. Once it is wrapped, with the stalk in your palm, just twizzle the stick a few times as this will help it hold together.

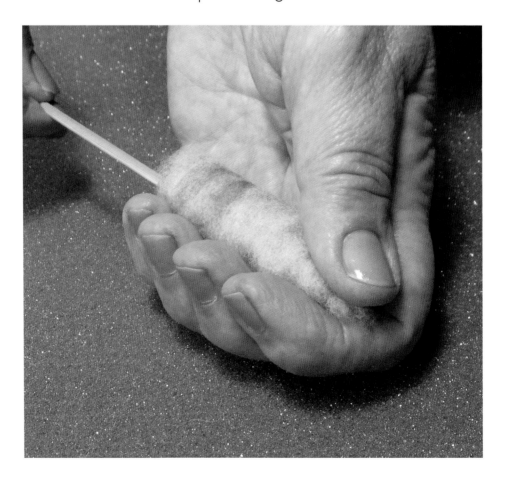

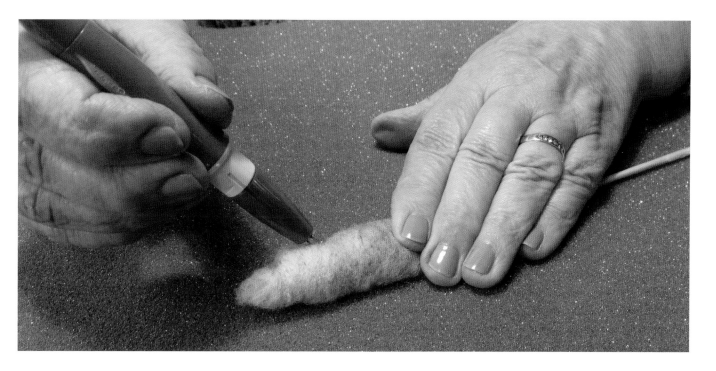

2. Lay the stick and wool back down on the pad, and very carefully felt the wool just a few times to make sure it is holding itself. Be careful not to hit the stick when doing this, as this will damage your needle.

3. Once you are happy the wool can hold itself, gently push it off the end of the skewer. DO NOT PULL IT OFF!

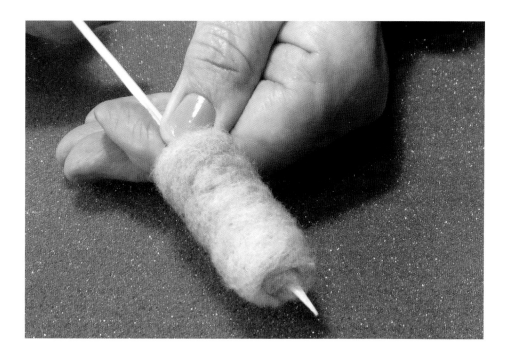

4. Now lay the stalk on your pad and felt it to firm it up. Also felt horizontally into the bottom of the stalk, leaving the other end loose and wispy to attach the toadstool cap.

5. Next, from the colour batting of your choice for your toadstool cap, pull off a piece of batting, approximately 11cm (4in) in diameter, and lay it on your pad. Then pull off two more identical pieces and stack them on top of one another.

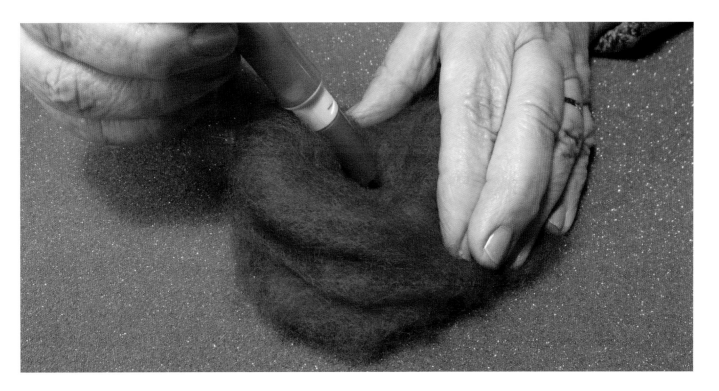

6. Now felt a 5cm (1.5in) circle in the middle of the wool pile. I would suggest using a multi tool for this stage, however, a single needle will also be fine, it will just take a little longer.

7. Next, gradually working your way around, fold the outside loose wool into the middle and felt it down, lifting and turning your work as you go.

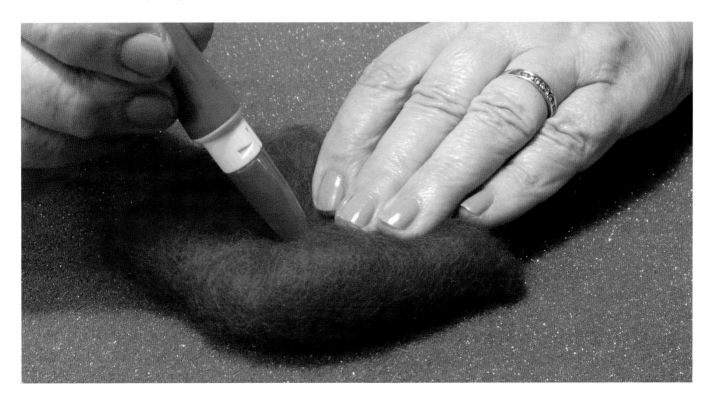

8. You should finally end up with a disc of felt, which you can then work your way around the edge to firm it up on by holding your fingers flat on top and felting into the edges.

9. Now plump up the height of your toadstool cap by adding a bit more wool on the top, keeping any wool you add towards the middle of the cap, and felt it on until it is firm.

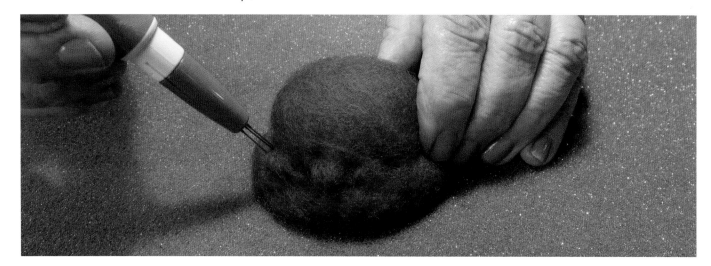

10. When you are happy with the size, add one last thin layer right over the cap and felt the complete piece all over until it is nice and smooth.

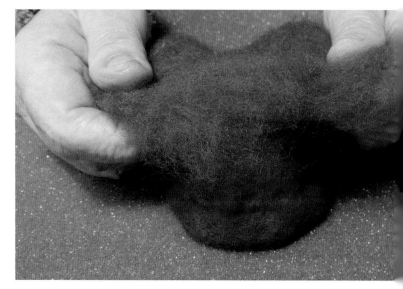

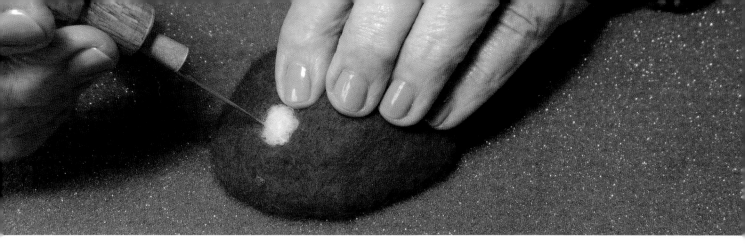

11. You can now add any features on the cap you wish, such as white spots, by taking small wisps of white wool and felting them on.

12. To fix your toadstool together, turn the cap upside down on your pad and put the wispy end of the stalk into the bottom of the cap. Felt these parts together, felting it all the way around until it feels secure.

13. To give a better finish, take small wisps of wool in your stalk colour and felt these over the join.

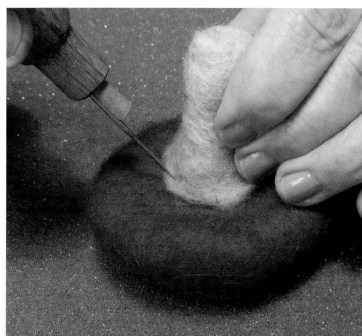

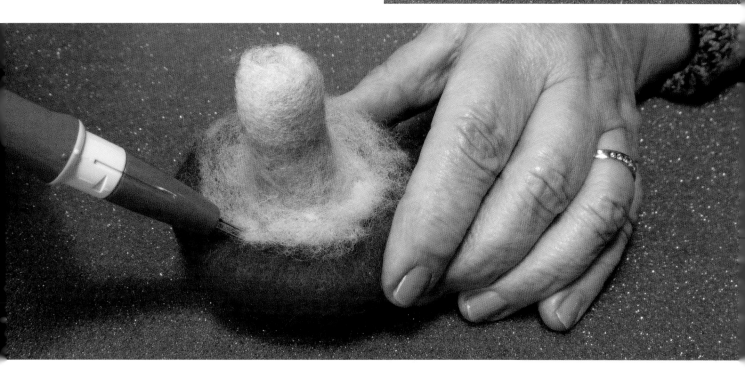

Once you have mastered these simple shapes, try making several more of varying sizes and colours to help you get used to the process and the feel of the needles and wool. Practice makes perfect.

The following pictures illustrate a few of the different things I have made using these simple shapes. I have made hearts into a brooch, a key ring and a magnet, and you could do the same with the flower. You can also thread any of the various shapes on to string and hang them from a ring or a branch, together with a fairy or two from Chapter 5, to make a mobile. Or by threading balls on to some string, together with some pretty beads maybe, make a necklace, bracelet or garland.

Finished Hearts.

Finished Toadstools.

Finished Ball Garland.

CHAPTER TWO

Buzzy Queen Bee and Beehive

A buzzy queen bee with her beehive, and a few of her worker bee friends!

Finished Queen Bee & Beehive.

For this chapter you will need:

- Core wool batting
- Carded wool batting in yellow, black, brown, pink and white
- 36/38/40/42 triangle single needles
- Multi tool
- Pair of 6mm black eyes
- Thin black wire
- 2 small black beads
- Optional white Angelina fibre
- Optional crown
- Wooden skewer

BEEHIVE

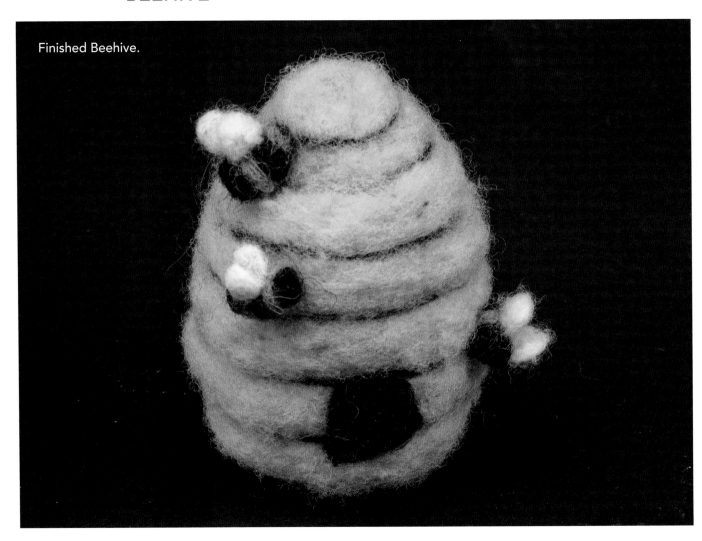

Finished Beehive.

1. Take a piece of core wool, approximately 31cm x 15cm (12in x 6in), and fold it in half lengthwise.

2. Next wrap the wool around the skewer as tightly as you can. It is important to get this as tight as you can from the start.

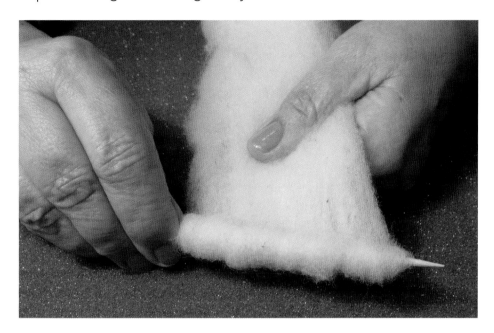

3. After you have started rolling, felt it with your needle (start with the coarser needles) and this will help stop it from unravelling. Continue rolling this up and once it is completely done, felt it a few times all over including at the top and bottom.

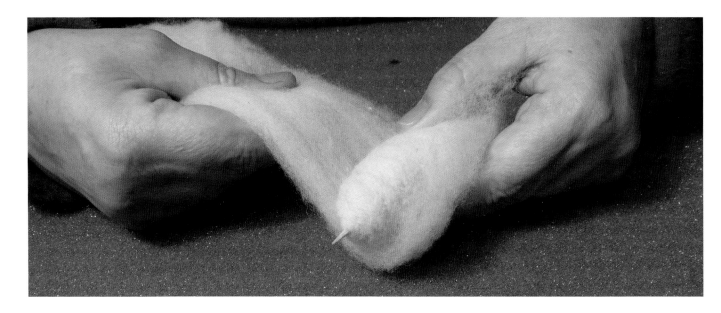

4. Now you will add another layer of wool, so take another piece of core wool, approximately 8cm x 21cm (3in x 8in), and wrap it around your started hive. Use your needle to felt and attach it.

5. Add another thin layer of core wool in the same way as step 4.

6. Next remove the beehive from the wooden skewer by pushing it up from the bottom, rather than pulling it from the top, otherwise you could find the middle stays wrapped around the stick!

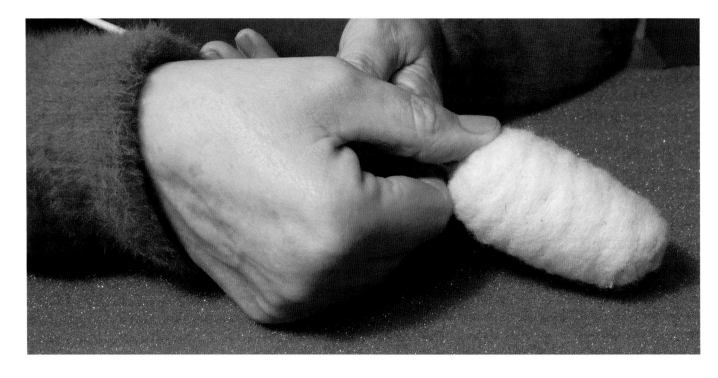

7. Once off the skewer, you now need to felt the top and bottom until smooth.

8. At this stage I usually like to add one more layer but just on the bottom half of the beehive to form a hive shape. To do this, take a strip long enough to wrap around the bottom a couple of times and just felt it down enough to hold it. The finished dome should be approximately 8cm x 6cm (3in x 2in), but the size isn't really that important and is up to personal preference.

9. Next take your yellow batting and pull off a strip large enough to cover and wrap around the dome twice, approximately 30cm x 13cm (12in x 5in). Make sure this isn't too thick, just enough to cover and not see the core wool underneath.

10. Lay your dome on top of the yellow wool and roll it up tightly. Felt down the loose edge first and then felt all around the sides, then the top and bottom of the hive, pulling off any excess wool as you go but leaving enough to cover the core. This is one of the final layers, so if you want your hive to be a bit larger at this stage then you can add another layer of yellow and repeat felting it down.

11. Take thin wisps of brown wool and tease them into long thin lines, and then twist them in between your fingers to make a thread.

12. Place your hive on your mat and lay the thread on to the beehive towards the bottom, then using either a 36 or 38 gauge single needle, felt it in a continuous line all the way around the beehive. I usually start felting at the bottom end of the hive, if the thread breaks off don't worry, just carry on laying the thread where it ended.

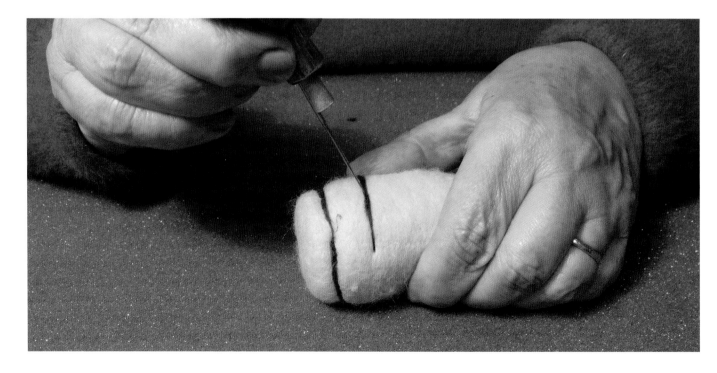

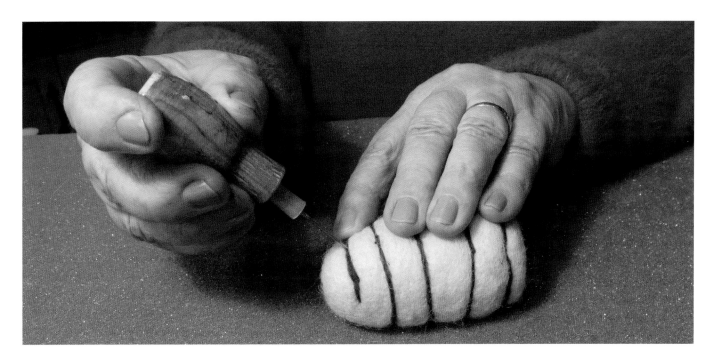

13. Add another line about 1.5cm (½in) above the previous one. Continue to add lines until you get to the top; this normally ends up around five lines.

14. Next take a small bit of the yellow wool and felt it into a loose ball shape. This can then be felted on to the top of the hive, then add a line of brown around the bottom of this also.

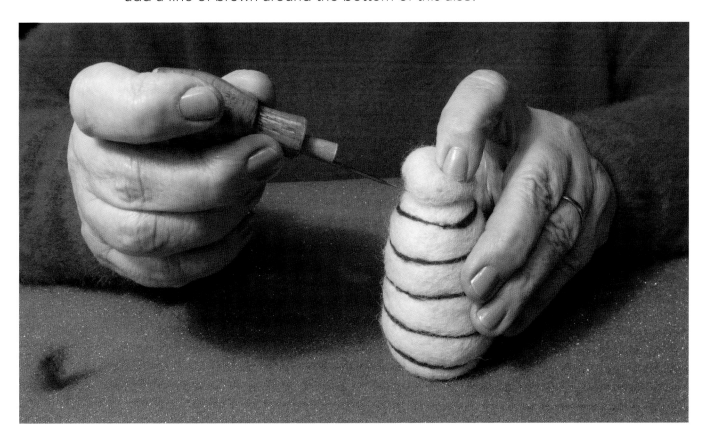

15. Now, take a small piece of brown wool and fold it into a rough doorway shape, about the size of your thumb pad, and felt this on to the hive wherever you decide is going to be the front.

16. The very last thing I like to do on the hive to finish it well, is to take small pieces of yellow wool and felt this on to the hive in between the brown lines loosely. You only need to attach this, rather than felt it down solid, as I feel gives it a little bit more texture. You could even use a slightly different shade of yellow if you have another one – or even mix two shades together.

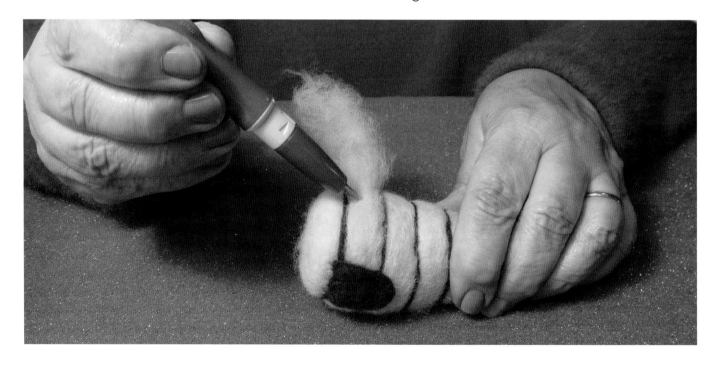

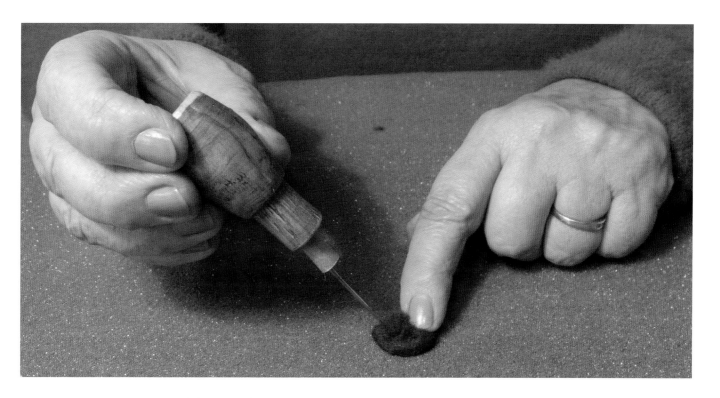

17. To add a small honeybee to the outside of the hive, take a tiny piece of brown wool and with your fingers roll it into a seed-like shape, then carefully felt it until firm. When felting something so tiny, take your time so you don't catch your fingers!

18. Now take a tiny wisp of yellow and roll it into a thin thread, wrap it around the tiny brown bee body and felt it on. Repeat, adding lines as you did with the hive; however, as these are tiny you will probably only get a couple of stripes on the body.

19. Next take a small piece of black wool and felt it on one end for the face.

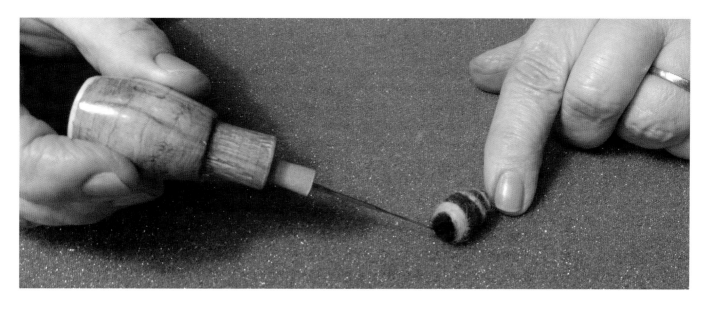

20. Now take two tiny, even-sized pieces of white wool. Felt them and encourage them into a wing shape, leaving one of the ends on each wing wispy, to attach it to the body. Once happy with these, felt the wings on the top of the tiny bee body one at a time.

21. To fix the tiny bee to the hive, use a dab of superglue. You can then repeat the process to add as many little bees to the hive as you want.

Finished Queen Bee.

QUEEN BUZZY BEE

1. Take a piece of core wool, approximately 18cm x 10cm (7in x 4in), and fold it into three lengthwise. Once folded, felt it a few times to stop it from unfolding.

2. Next roll it up tightly, then felt the ends down so it won't unroll again.

3. Now felt the wool all over, turning it as you felt. Decide which end is slightly fatter, as you will make that end the face. It often naturally forms a cone shape, so the aim here is for one end to gradually tail off to a rounded point and the other end will be the wider, flatter end which you will use for the face, so you need work on achieving that shape as you felt.

4. Keep felting this until it is firm and in a cone shape, felting the face flat. It should finish up about 6cm x 3cm (2in x 1in).

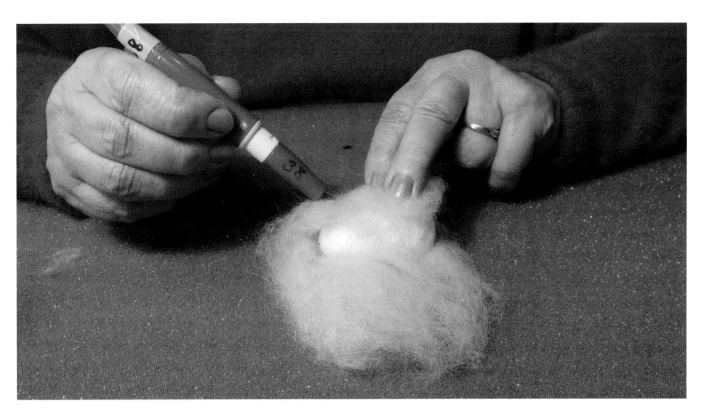

5. Now take a piece of yellow batting large enough to wrap around the body. Lay the body on the yellow wool and wrap it around, then felt the yellow wool down to secure. You may find once you have wrapped it around that you have an excess of wool at the ends, and as you don't want it to be too bulky, you can just pull off the excess, leaving enough to cover the ends.

6. Now add the face using a contrasting colour, either black or brown, by taking a small piece of wool and felting a layer over the face end.

7. Next take some brown or black wool and pull off some thin strips to add to the bee for the stripes. Starting at the face end, wrap a black or brown strip around the body and felt this on enough to attach and hold it on to the queen bee.

8. Now repeat, adding stripes along the body, leaving gaps between to show the yellow body colour. There should be room for the bee to have two or three bands, depending on how thick you have done them.

9. Like you did with the beehive, now take some small pieces of yellow wool and felt these on to the yellow parts of the body to give your bee a fuzzy look and nice texture. Skip this part if you want it smooth.

10. Take a small piece of white wool and felt this into the very end of the body on her bum!

11. Now you can add some features to your bee's face. Remember, if you felt something in and you decide it isn't quite in the right place, then simply pull it out and have another try. If you are using glass eyes, they should have a stalk on them for attaching to your bee. With the awl, make a deep hole for the stalks one at a time, checking you are happy with the position. Dab a little glue on the stalk ends and carefully push them in, holding them in tightly until the glue takes hold. If you haven't any glass eyes, you can felt in two small eyes using wool and a single needle.

12. Taking a small wisp of white, twist this in your fingers to make a thread, and felt this on to the face to make her mouth, snipping off any excess thread with scissors. You could also add a wisp of pink wool felted in lightly for the cheeks.

13. To make the wings you will need to pull off two small thin pieces of white wool, a little larger than the size of a 2p coin. Lay out your wool wings and get them as near to the same size as possible, slightly wider at one end, leaving the other end wispy for attaching to the body.

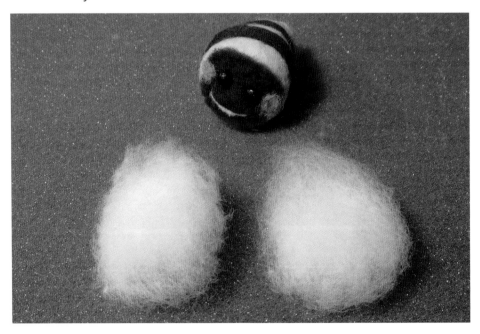

14. Using your punch or multi tool, felt the wings just a little to start with, tidying the edges by pulling any stray fibres inwards. If you are adding some Angelina fibre, take a small piece of this and either pull or snip off some fibres so they lie on top of the wings. Then take a miniscule amount of white wool and lay this over the Angelina on the wing and carefully felt down. Angelina fibre is a man-made product and doesn't felt, which is why it needs to be anchored down with some more wool. The top layer of wool needs to be very thin so that when felted you can still see the Angelina shimmer.

15. Turn the wing over and repeat step 14 on the back of the wing. At this stage, you can trim off any stray bits if you wish, or just leave them if you prefer.

16. Now with a single needle, felt each wing on to the back of the bee by holding it in place, and felting the loose fibres from the wispy end of the wing into the body, positioned nearer to the head than the tail.

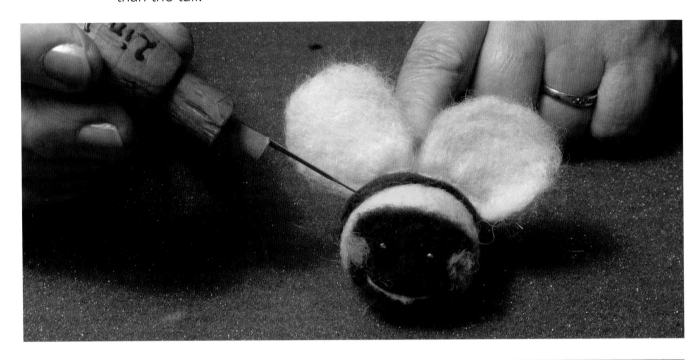

17. Take the thin black wire, cut two small pieces for the antenna, long enough to allow for part of them to fix into the body once you have decided how long you want these to be. Then using superglue, add a small black bead to the end of each antenna.

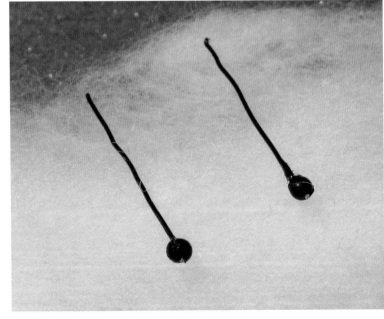

18. Make two holes, one each side of the head, using your awl. Put a dab of superglue on the bottom of each antenna and push these into the holes as deep as you need to get them the right length. Felt in the hole around the wire, using a little of the matching colour of wool to hold it securely.

19. An optional extra to finish the project is to superglue a little gold crown on the top of her head if you wish. These are easily purchased online.

Finished Queen Bee Flying.

CHAPTER THREE

Fun, Fantasy Owl

A cute fun, fantasy owl that can be made in a variety of colours.

For this chapter you will need:

- Core wool batting
- Carded wool batting in your colour choices
- Mixture of needles (36/38/40/42 gauges)
- Pair of glass or acrylic eyes OR black carded wool batting
- White carded wool batting
- Wool Nepps and Angelina fibre (optional)
- Wooden skewer
- For this owl I have used Living Felt CW-1 core wool and their MC-1 wool batting (colours Fall Goody Bag) both of which are their own special blend of wool. It is so wonderfully soft, and felts very easily.

1. Firstly, you need to build up a firm dense cone shape on the wooden skewer, which will be the main body of the owl. Taking your core wool, pull off some thin strips of about 2.5cm (1in) wide. Hold the wool on the skewer with your fingers and thumb in one hand and turn the skewer with your other hand, holding the wool with your thumb quite firmly to help keep this as tight as possible. Wrap down the skewer to around 8cm (3in) taking care not to let the wool slide further down the skewer than you want by holding your fingers on the skewer at the end of where you want it to stop.

2. Once you have wrapped down the skewer, then wrap the wool back over what you have just wrapped, up to just slightly higher than the point of the stick.

3. Once you have wrapped a layer on, use a single needle (36 or 38 gauge) and felt firmly at an angle each side of the skewer, taking

Finished Owl

care to avoid hitting the stick and breaking the needle. This will hold the wool and stop it from unrolling, and by felting it firmly in the middle it will help give you a nice, firm inner body.

4. Repeat wrapping strips on to your body and ensure after wrapping you felt each layer well. Keep repeating until the inner body is approx. 3.5–5cm (1.5–2in) in diameter, or however plump you want your owl to be. It may only be two or three layers, but this will depend on your core wool and how thin your strips are, so this is up to the individual to decide.

5. Now, leaving the core wool body on the stick, felt the loose wool at the top into a dome shape.

6. Next push the dome off the skewer from the bottom; it is best not to pull it off as you risk leaving the middle of dome behind when you pull.

7. From your chosen colour of carded wool batting, pull off a wide strip, large enough in size to go completely around your owl's body with a slight overlap. Wrap the batting around your owl's body and using your Clover pen, or any multi tool, felt the coloured batting on to the dome at the sides first to attach the wool, turning the body as you go.

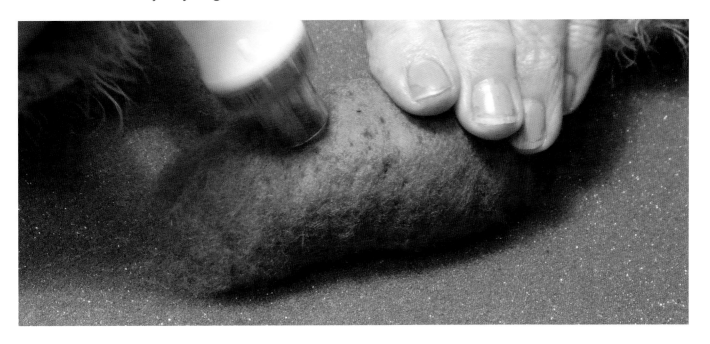

8. On the ends of the dome, you need enough coloured wool batting to cover them although not so much that you add a lot of bulk there, so you will have to judge this and pull off any excess wool. Don't worry if you pull too much off, you can easily patch it up again. Felt both the ends down making sure you keep a nice flat bottom and dome shape at the top.

9. Next check the body is fully covered; you can patch any thin areas with more wool or even add another thin layer if you feel it needs it. Then felt all over the body surface, making it as smooth as you can by going over it with a fine needle and felting any bumps down. Both the Clover pen and punch tools work well for this.

10. Now I like to add the eyes. Start by felting two small white circles flat on your pad. You can experiment with the size, but mine are about 1.5cm (0.5in) in diameter.

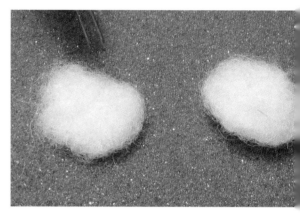

11. Now lay these on to the body, just slightly down from the top. I place them so they meet in the middle but don't overlap. Felt them on to the body, working around the edge of the circles as these are just bases for the eyes.

12. I like to use glass or plastic eyes, which you can purchase online easily, either plain black or coloured, and you can even purchase eyes made especially for owls. Here I have used 12mm orange owl eyes. With your awl, make a hole in each of the white circles so that the eyes sit almost, but not quite, touching. Don't

worry if you get it wrong and you need to move the hole, as that will get covered anyway, but you can always needle some more white wool into the hole you don't want. When you are happy with the position, add a drop of glue to the stalks on the back of the eyes and push them in. (If you are not using this type of eye then you can felt a smaller circle of orange or yellow on to the white circles with a black centre felted in.)

13. Now you can enhance the eye by felting some wool around it. Take a colour wool batting of your choice and pull off two small, thin strips, long enough to make a circle around each eye. Roll the strip on your pad with your fingers to form it into a sausage-like strip and felt this a little, just enough to hold it and stop it from unrolling.

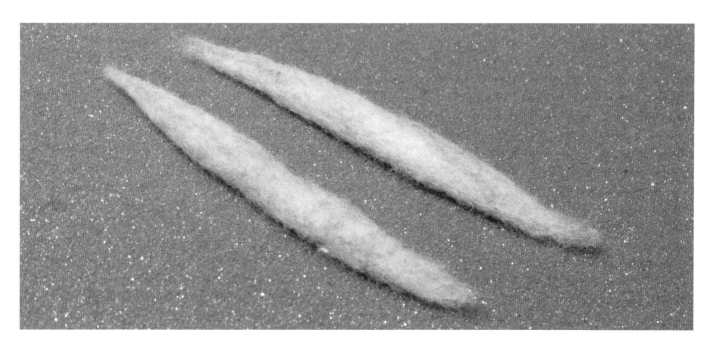

14. Taking one strip at a time, carefully felt it in a circle around each eye, just enough to attach to the owl so it stands out around the eye. Pull or snip off any excess wool.

15. Taking another contrasting colour, pull off two very thin wisps, roll them in your fingers and needle them around the outside of the eyes to frame them.

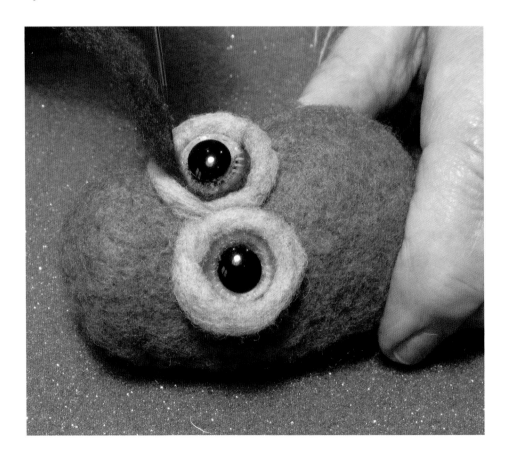

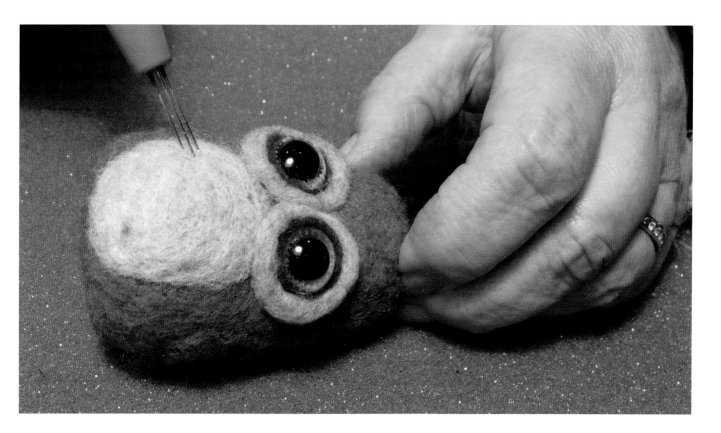

16. Moving on, take your chosen tummy colour wool batting and tear off a small thin piece and form it into either a circle or oval depending on your personal preference, either felting from under the eyes down to the base with the oval shape or just a small circle piece in the middle of the owl's tummy.

17. If you have chosen to use any 'bling' fibre, like wool nepps or Angelina, you can add this to the tummy now. Neither of these two fibres will felt, so to add them you need to mix them in a little wool.

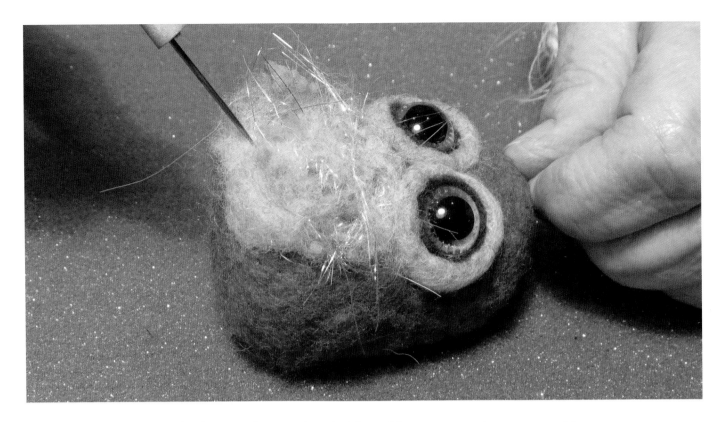

18. Felt the wool mixed with bling fibres on to the tummy. Here I have added both nepps and Angelina fibre using some carded wool batting. You can trim away any pieces of bling sticking out once you have it felted on.

19. Now you will add an outline around the tummy in a contrasting colour, in the same way as outlining the eyes.

20. For the beak, choose your colour wool batting and, taking a small wisp, wrap it around the very tip of the wooden skewer, being careful to not let it get too long, but you can practise this until you get the size of beak that you want. Carefully felt the wool on the skewer, just enough so that it doesn't unroll.

21. Push the beak off the skewer from the bottom, then felt it a little more until it is nice and firm, but be sure to leave a few wispy fibres at the base, for attaching it to the owl.

22. Hold the base of the beak on the owl's face, low down between the eyes, and felt this on using the wispy fibres left on the base, working your way all around the beak.

23. This next step is optional. You can leave the beak as it is, or at the very end point of the beak you can bend it downwards and felt it on to the face further down.

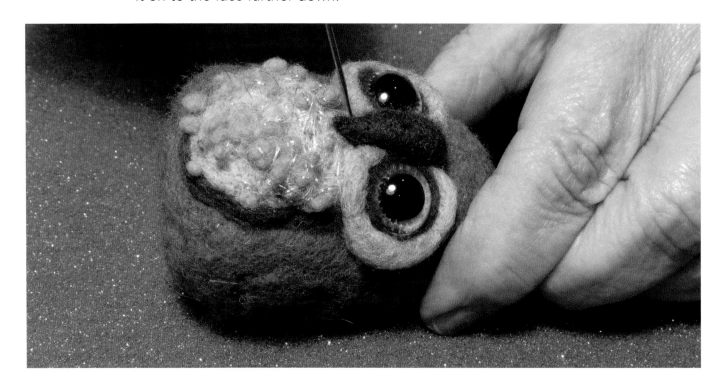

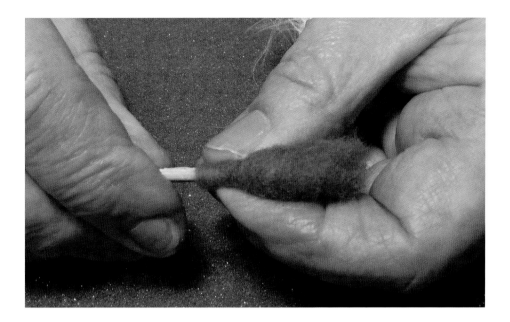

24. Now you can add the ears or horns. You can use whichever colour wool batting you wish and make them to any size you want. To make these, pull off two wisps of wool and one at a time wrap them into a cone shape on the end of the skewer. The pointed end of the skewer is the base of the ear.

25. Turn the skewer in your fingers, and the warmth from your fingers will felt the wool enough to hold it while you remove it from the skewer. Once removed, place the ear on your mat and felt the point of the ear first, by felting it from the outside using shallow stabs to make the point of the ear sharp and precise. Turn the ear the other way and felt into the point from the inside as well to firm it up. Felt the ear all over as well, leaving some wisps at the bottom for attaching to the owl.

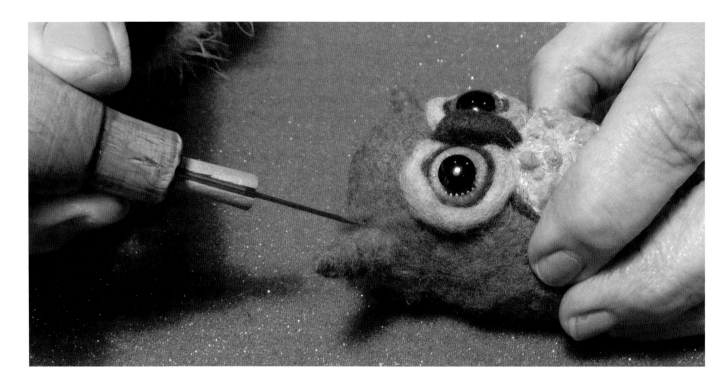

26. Now you can fix the ears to the owl. Place the ears on the top of the head at each side and felt them on using the wispy ends left at the base of the ears to attach them. If you can still see joins around them anywhere, take very tiny wisps of wool and lay them over the joint areas and felt them over the top.

27. Next the wings; there are two ways of adding these to your owl. The first option is to take some wool batting in your choice of colour and pull off two pieces of wool. This will be folded over to make the wing so pull off enough to allow for this. Felt the pieces just very lightly now, one at a time, fold the wool in half and lay it on to the side of the owl with the folded side at the top.

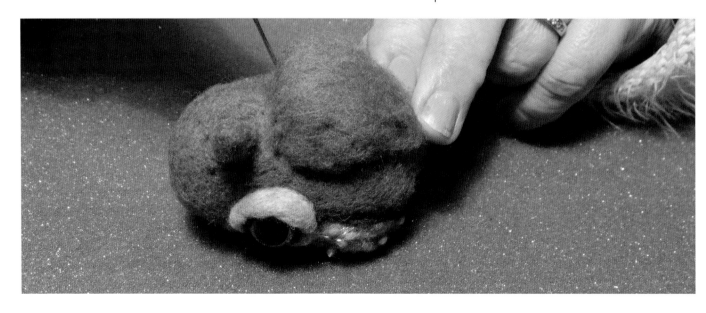

28. With a single needle, either a 36 or 38 gauge, attach each wing to the owl by felting it on, starting first at the top and working your way completely around the outside of the wing, tucking in any wispy bits sticking out and then lightly felt over the wing leaving the middle so it sits out proud from the body.

29. If preferred, you can leave the wings loose by the owl's side. For this option, pull off the same amount of wool, lightly felt and fold it over as in the first option, but this time felt the wing flat on your pad with your Clover punch tool or multi needle, leaving the folded end a bit wispy for attaching. Carefully neaten up the edges of the wings by folding them in and felting the edges down. Now attach each wing to the owl by felting just at the top of the wing and felt a little way down the sides, this way it will leave the bottom part of the wing loose from the body.

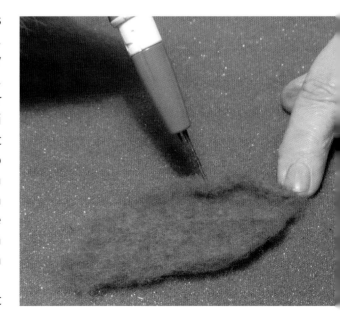

30. So that your owl will stand up, felt

a small disc of wool with your punch tool to get a nice flat solid shape, tidying up the edges with a single needle. Felt the disc on to the bottom of the owl so it is secure and flat. Then with a single needle, felt an indentation at the front of the base in the middle to separate it slightly, into the appearance of two feet. Alternatively, you could glue the owl on to a base of some kind, such as a wood slice purchased easily online.

Owl chapter inspired by Marie Spaulding of Living Felt – link to their fantasy owl is:
www.livingfelt.com/fantasyowls

Owl by Marie Spaulding of Living Felt.

Finished Owls.

CHAPTER FOUR

Cheeky Mouse

A cheeky little mouse.

To make your mouse, you will need:

- Your choice of mouse colour brown/grey/white carded batt OR carded merino wool batt (I use merino carded wool for mice, as it gives a soft velvet look, but any carded wool will be fine)
- Carded core wool
- Flesh and white carded wool small amount
- 2 x 30cm (12in) pipe cleaners
- 7mm black glass eyes or black beads
- Whiskers (horse hair or nylon thread)

1. First make the body shape. Take a piece of carded core wool, approximately 20cm x 10cm (8in x 4in), and lay this lengthways on your mat. Fold the outer side edges in to make the wool approximately 7.5cm (3in) wide. Now, roll the wool up as tightly as you can. Felt the join to stop it unrolling.

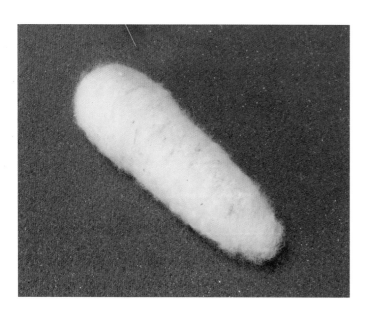

2. Next felt this all over. One end needs to be more pointed and the other wider end flat, so as you felt, work on forming this into a cone shape. Once felted, the cone shape should be approximately 7.5cm (3in) tall by 2.5cm (1in) in diameter.

3. Wrap another layer of core wool around the cone and felt this in.

4. Then wrap another layer of

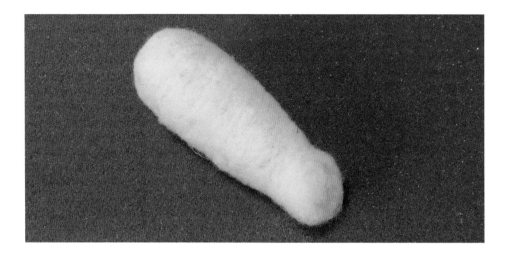

core wool on the bottom half only, so the bottom is larger than the rest of the body. Put this aside for now.

5. Now you will make the head shape. Take a small strip of carded core wool, approximately 6cm x 20cm (2in x 8in), and fold it in three widthways. Roll this up tightly and felt the join to stop it unrolling. Felt the ends next as this will help keep the head in shape. Then felt the head all over until it is firm. If there is one end that seems thicker than the other, then work this end rounded for the back of the head and felt the thinner end into a point for the nose. Otherwise, just choose an end for each and work it in the same way.

6. Hold the head on the body to judge the size. If you think it looks a bit small, you can add another thin layer over and felt it, but don't add too much extra to the length of the head.

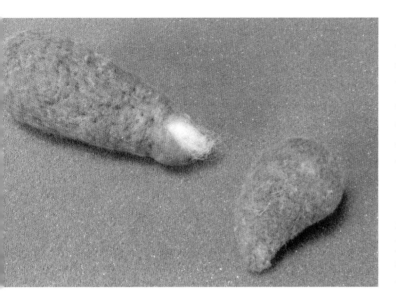

7. Now cover the head and body in your choice of coloured topcoat wool, taking small pieces of wool at a time and felting it on firmly enough to attach it to the core wool. Leave some wispy wool to use for attaching the head on the top of the body. If you can see the core wool showing through in places you can just patch it up with small wisps of wool felted on top of the thin areas.

8. Fan out the wispy wool at the top of the body and, holding the head on top, felt them together. Needle the loose wool on the body into the head, working your way around to attach them together.

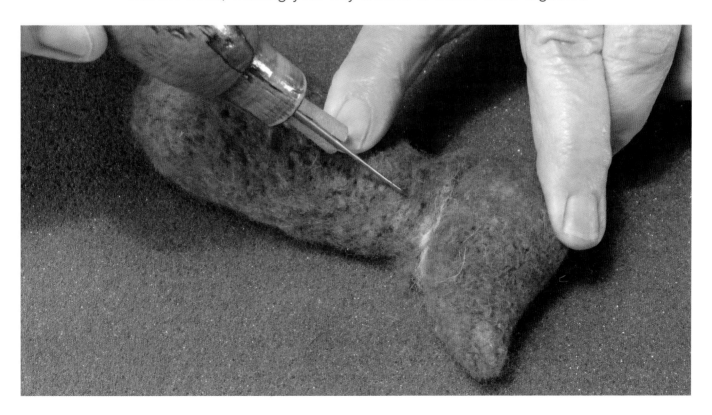

You can pose your head now by moving it into the angle you want – for example if you want it looking slightly upwards, move it to the desired position and hold it there while you felt downwards from the head into the back of the neck; this will shorten it, leaving the nose pointing upwards.

9. Now lay small wisps of wool vertically over the neck join and felt them well to secure this and cover the join.

10. Take a 30cm (12in) pipe cleaner and cut in half, one piece for each back leg. Bend it in half and lightly twist it, and then bend 2.5cm (1in) up for the foot.

11. Wrap the foot and leg with a thin piece of flesh-coloured carded wool. Add another wrap just over the foot to make this slightly thicker, but don't let it get too big. The best way to wrap the foot is to wrap from the leg end towards the toe of the foot. To wrap the toe, wind the wool in a figure of eight just back from the very tip; this will help keep the wool from slipping off the end. Using a fine needle, felt it firmly, being careful to avoid hitting the wire. Repeat these steps for the other leg.

12. Take a small piece of topcoat coloured wool and loosely wrap it around the top half of the leg only and felt it flat. This will give you the mouse's thigh, which you will use to attach the leg to the body.

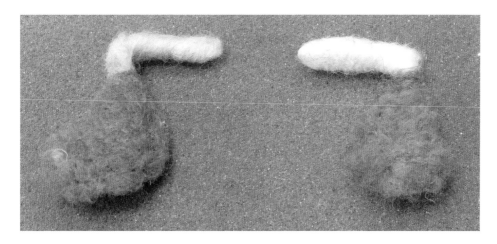

13. Place the leg on the body so that the foot sits level or very slightly lower than the body and felt through the thigh and into the body until it holds firmly. Attach the other leg in the same way.

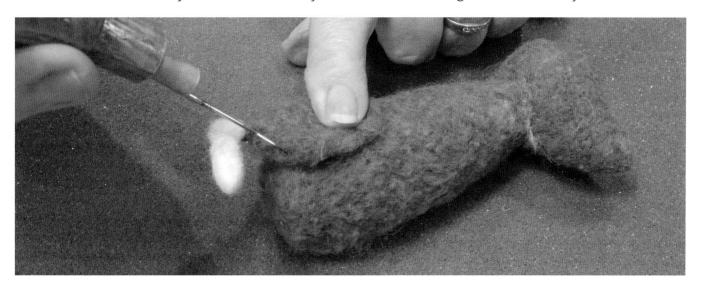

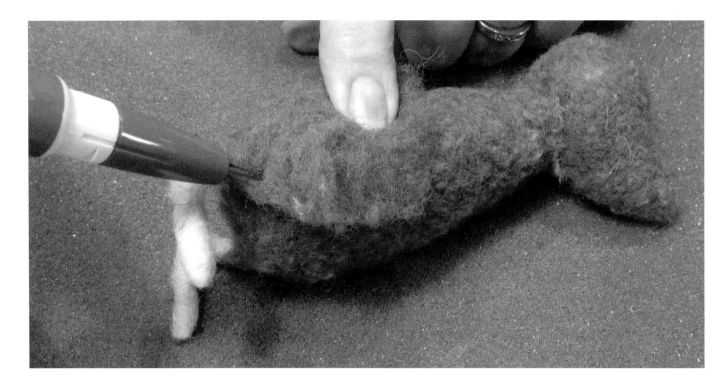

Once they are both firmly felted on, lay a small piece of wool batt over the whole thigh area and felt it down, to build the area up and cover any joins.

14. Cut another 30cm (12in) pipe cleaner in half; one half will be the tail, and the other half will be for the top legs.

15. For the top legs, take one half of the pipe cleaner and cut this in half. Bend each section in half and twist the wires slightly – not too much or they will be too short.

16. Wrap the folded end using the same method as for the toes, with a wisp of flesh-coloured wool, and felt firmly. Then cover the rest of the leg in the topcoat coloured wool, leaving some loose wool at the other end of the leg to attach to the body.

17. Attach these either side of the body just slightly down from the head by felting the loose wool around the top of the leg into the body, avoiding the wire. Then if you are happy with the placing of the legs, take wisps of topcoat coloured wool, lay them over the joints, and felt them to secure the legs on. If you want to change the position, before adding more wool, pull the legs off carefully, re-attach them in the new position and then cover the joints.

18. Now to make the tail. Take the other half of the pipe cleaner and fold the end over so your tail is approximately 8–10cm (3–4in) long. The thicker end will be the end you attach to the body. Take long thin wisps of flesh-coloured wool and wrap them around the pipe cleaner. The best way to do this is by using your thumb and index finger to smooth the wool as you wrap it around the pipe cleaner, turning the pipe cleaner with your other hand, and felting each wisp on as you go. Make the tip thinner and gradually thicken the tail as you move towards the body end, by not adding as much wool at the tip. Make sure you leave the thicker end slightly wispy for attaching it to your mouse.

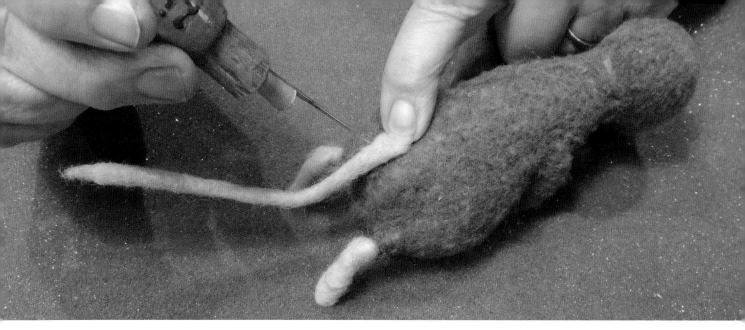

19. Lay your mouse on the pad and place just under 2cm (1in) of the tail on the mouse's back at the bottom. Felt the loose ends into the body well so it holds really firmly. Sit the mouse up and bend the tail to check it is in the correct position, as the tail is used to balance the mouse and hold it upright. Fiddle with the tail positioning until the mouse stands upright. If he tips back, it maybe because the tail is sitting a bit too high on his back; if this is the case you can remove the tail and re-attach it. Once you are happy that he is standing well and your tail is in the correct position, take wisps of topcoat wool and lay them over the join from all angles around the tail, and felt some wool in close around the tail to keep it tight.

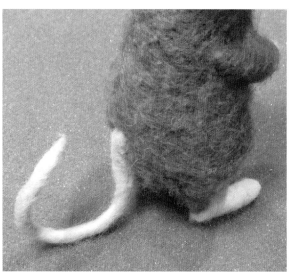

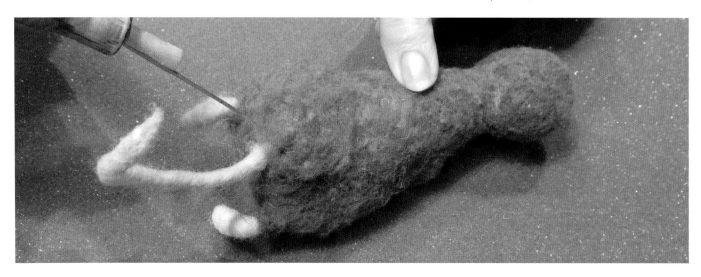

20. Now look at your mouse and see if anywhere needs building up, perhaps giving it a fatter bottom, bulking out the thighs, giving it a bigger tummy, covering your joins etc. All these things can be done by taking small pieces of wool and felting them on. When you are bulking it out, the aim is to just attach it and shape it; you don't need to make it really solid, as it has no purpose other than for the look you want to achieve. To do this, work on it sufficiently to ensure it is felted on but leave enough volume to add the bulk and shape you require.

21. For the ears, take two pieces of flesh-coloured wool of the same size and about twice the size you want the ears to be. Your punch tool is ideal for this part if you have one, if not use a multi tool or single needle. Felt the ears on your pad, remembering to lift them off your pad occasionally. Once they start to flatten, fold the edges in to form the size ear you require so you get a nice rim around the outside of the ear and felt it down. Mice ears are very thin so try not to make them too thick. Leave the bottom of the ears wispy for attaching.

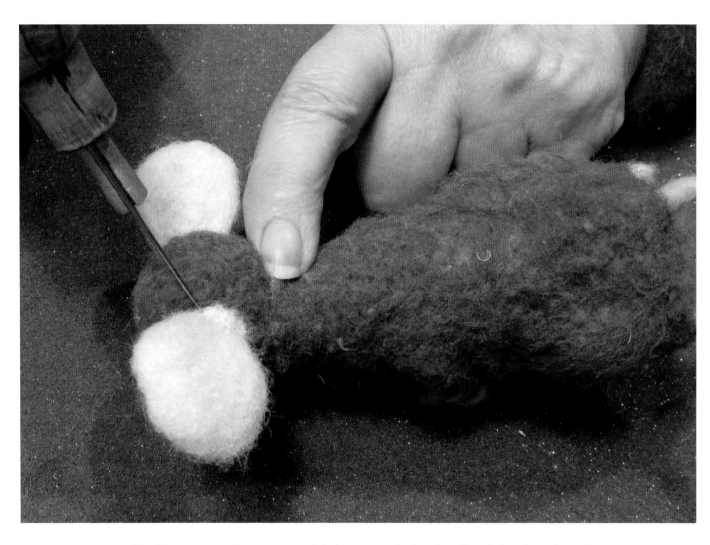

22. To attach the ears, hold them near the back of the head and slightly to the sides, then felt the wispy ends into the head.

23. Before you add the nose and eyes, decide if you are happy with the head shape. On my mouse I took two fluffy balls of topcoat wool and felted them on to the side of the face to give him chubbier cheeks, but you can add small wisps of wool anywhere you think it needs it.

24. To create the nose, take a small piece of flesh-coloured wool, fold it into a tiny triangle shape, carefully lay it on the tip of the nose, and felt it on, working just around the outside edge of the triangle shape to attach it. Take two wisps of white wool and roll them

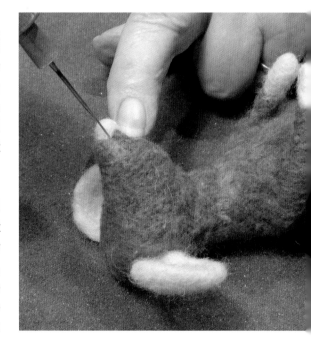

into little soft balls, and felt these just below and either side of the nose.

25. If you are using glass eyes, use your awl to make two holes, about halfway between the ears and the nose and towards the sides. Check you are happy with the position, then add a dab of glue on

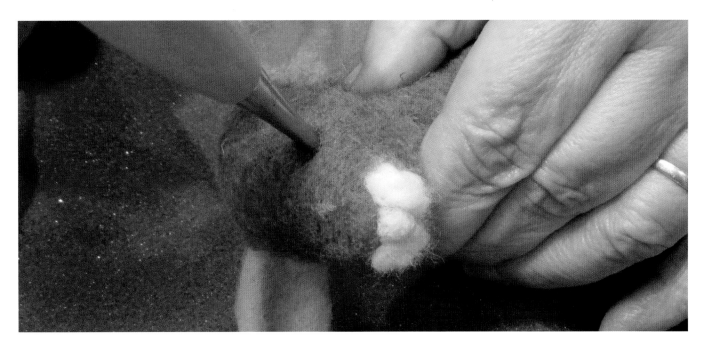

the stalk of each eye and push them into the holes. Or you can sew black beads on for the eyes. To do this, I would stab an indentation in the position of the eyes first, using a single needle, and then sew the beads in, pulling them up tightly so they get embedded into the head. When the mouse's eyes (whichever method) are in place, take a tiny wisp of white wool, twist it in your fingers to make a thread and felt this in around the eye.

26. Add the whiskers by threading them through with a needle from one side to the other. Add a tiny dab of glue on the area that will be pulled into the muzzle.

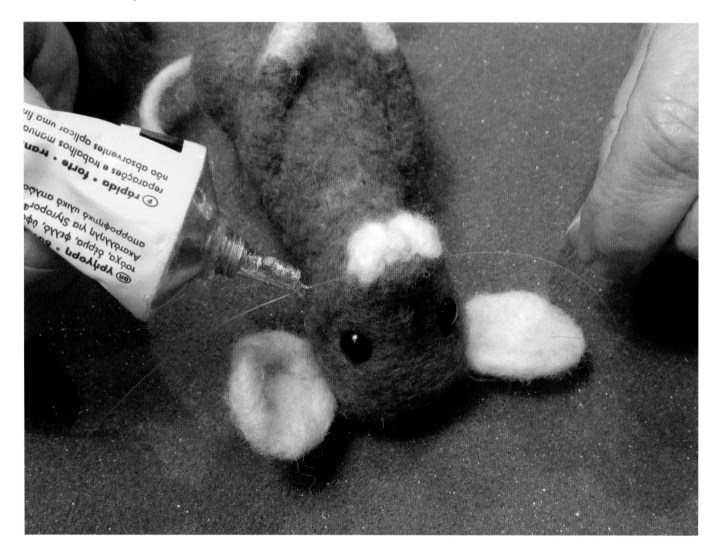

27. For a finishing touch, you could add some white wool on to his chest.

CHAPTER FIVE

Fairy

A magical, pretty fairy, this could also be made into a witch.

To make your fairy, you will need:

- 2 x 30cm (12in) pipe cleaners
- Dyed wool locks or wool tops for hair in colour of your choice
- White wool tops for wings
- Flesh-coloured carded wool batt
- Carded wool batts in your choice of colours for dress

1. Take one pipe cleaner and fold it in half and make a small loop at the top by twisting it three times. This will be the head, the neck and the arms.

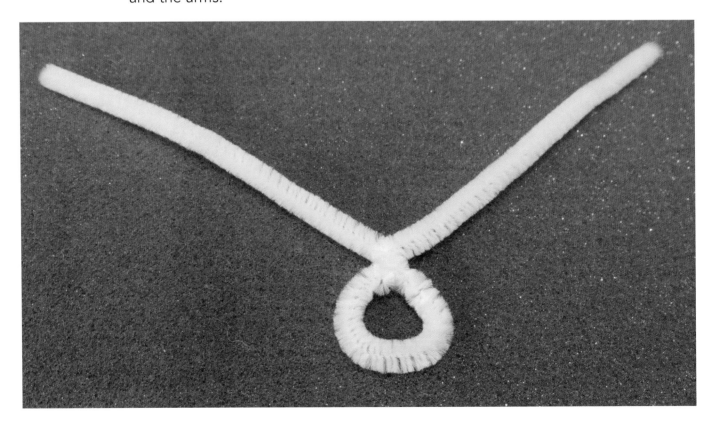

Finished Fairy.

Finished Witch.

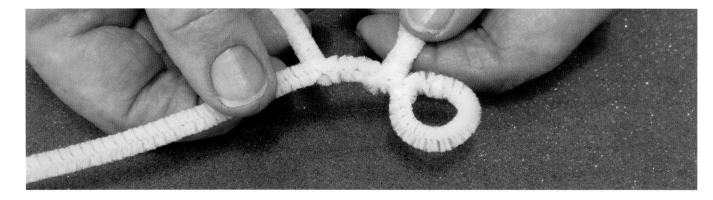

2. Take the second pipe cleaner and fold in half. Place this over the neck part of the first pipe cleaner. Twist the pipe cleaners together to each side of the neck to form the shoulders.

3. Make the body by bringing the two ends together and twist these together two or three times.

4. Bend and fold over about 2.5cm (1") at the ends of both the arms and legs so the sharp ends of the pipe cleaners are folded in. You should now have your fairy framework.

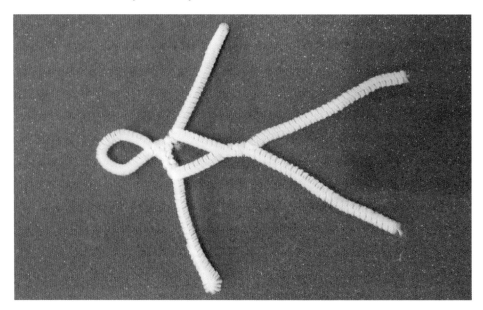

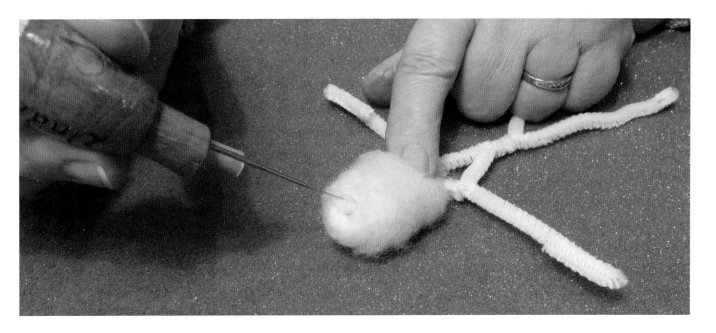

5. Take a thin 2.5cm (1in) wide strip of flesh-coloured carded wool, long enough to wrap the head two or three times. Wrap it around and felt it to hold it, then start to shape the head by felting the wool into a ball shape, taking care not to catch the wire with your needle.

6. Now you need to build up the face shape. To do this, take a small piece of flesh-coloured wool, fold it into a wad the size of the face, position it and felt it on to the face, starting with the edges first. Don't flatten the face down completely, work it just enough to felt it. Use a fine needle to needle felt and smooth the face over. You can add a wrap of wool around it and felt it down if you find it is still a bit bumpy.

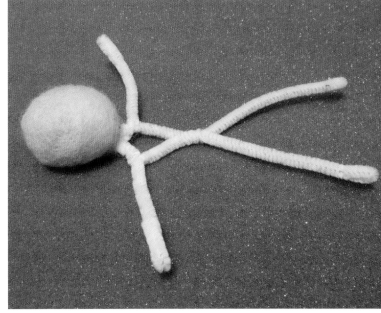

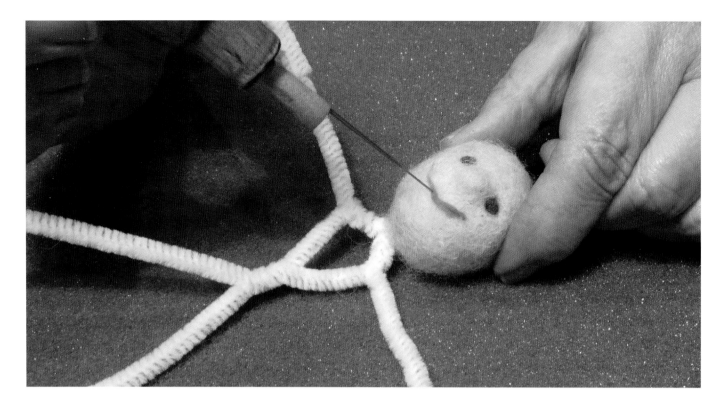

7. You now need to add the nose, the eyes and mouth. Take a wisp of flesh-coloured wool and roll it between your fingers to make a very tiny ball for the nose and carefully felt this on to the face. You can then add a tiny wisp over the nose to cover the joins. For the eyes, take a tiny amount of brown or blue wool and felt this on for the eyes. You can then add a small mouth with pink or red.

8. Now you can form the chin area into the shape you would like, you may like it to be pointy rather than round. Add a small ball of wool in the chin area if you want it pronounced then felt it and lay over a small wisp to cover any joins.

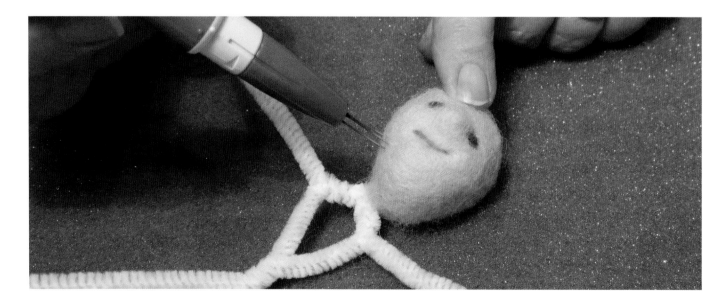

9. Take a small wisp of flesh-coloured wool and wrap the ends of the arms for the hands. Keep the wisps small, as you are better to add thin layers to build them up to avoid big, bulky hands – it isn't easy to remove once you have put it on! Felt the hands using a fine needle.

10. Tear off long, thin, narrow strips of flesh-coloured wool for the legs. Attach a strip on the body and then holding the strip firmly between your thumb and finger, turn the fairy so the wool gradually wraps around the leg moving downwards to the foot. Once covered, felt the leg with a single needle to tidy and smooth it. Take care here and only put the needle into the wool; try not to push the needle so far that it comes out of the other side, as this will push fibres out to the outside of the leg and make it wispy and not smooth. Repeat for other leg.

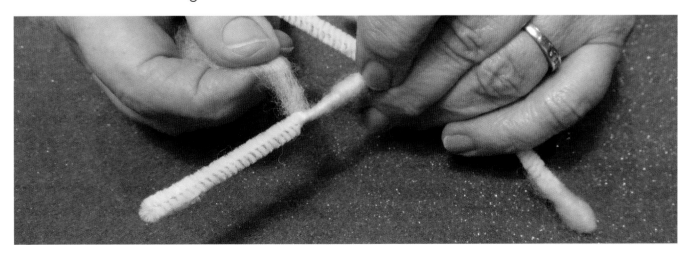

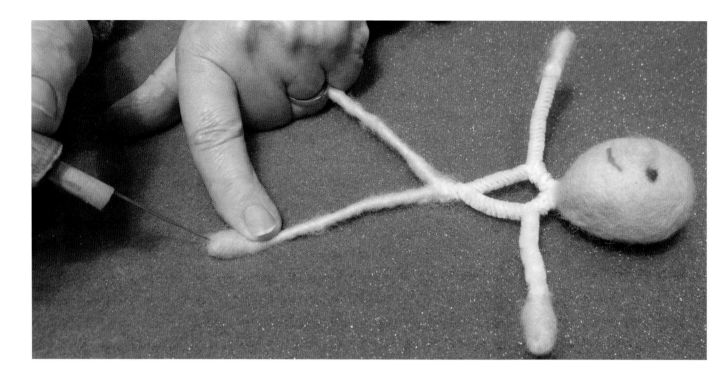

11. Now we will add the shoes, so choose your shoe colour and taking a small strip, wrap this around the very end of the legs and felt it until nice and smooth.

12. Take a strip of flesh-coloured wool about 1cm (½in) wide to wrap the neck and shoulders. Start by wrapping the neck first and then the shoulders, in a figure of eight movement once or twice around the neck; this should be nearly enough to cover the areas, but the shoulders may need an extra wrap. Felt slightly to hold this.

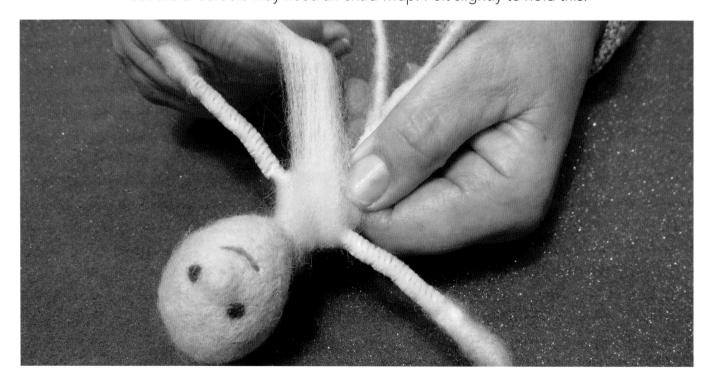

13. Now you will wrap the body. Pull off a few strips, as you will need a few to get the body filled out well. Wrap the body with the strips, being careful not to leave the waist too skinny, as you will need some wool there to attach the skirt. Felt slightly to hold.

14. At the very bottom of the body, you can wrap and felt a layer of colour over it so that from below the skirt it looks like she is wearing knickers. Do this by wrapping a thin layer of wool in a figure of eight around the top of the legs and then up around the bottom, finishing by felting to secure.

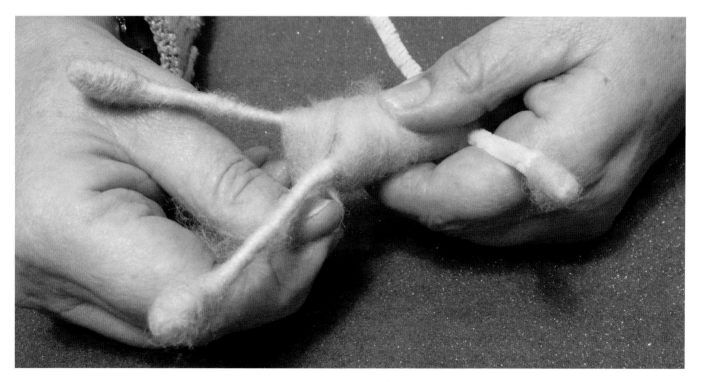

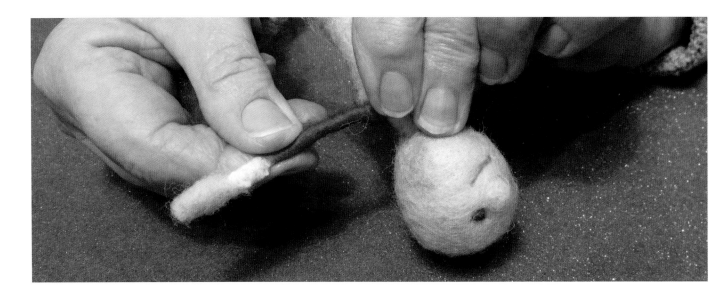

15. Decide on your colours for the bodice, the sleeves and skirt. These can be different or they can be all the same colour, it is entirely your choice. Take a thin strip of your sleeve colour wool, attach it at the back on the shoulder to hold it, and then, holding your finger and thumb on it, tightly wrap it around the arm down to the hand, in the same way you wrapped the legs. Pull off any excess wool and then felt it to hold. If you think the arm isn't thick enough, add another thin layer. Felt it until it is smooth, again taking care not to poke through to the other side.

16. To wrap the bodice, take a thin strip of your chosen wool, no more than 2.5cm (1in) wide and, starting at the neck, hold the wool at the back with your finger and thumb and tightly wrap the wool in a figure of eight around the shoulders just the same as you did the flesh-coloured layer. Work your way down to the waist and lightly felt it to hold. You can leave the neck flesh-coloured or you can wrap

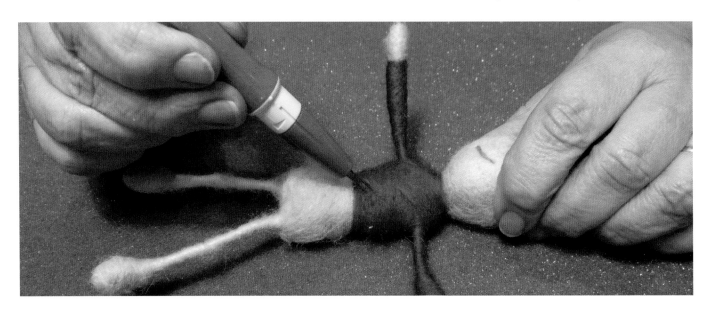

it in the same colour as the bodice. You can now add another layer to build the bodice up or you can leave it as it is; this will depend on how much wool you put on the first wrap and whether you want a slim or plump fairy. This is what I enjoy about creating, as you can make your fairy as you see it or want it to be.

17. Now for the skirt, which you will make up using some petal shapes, meaning you can use one colour or as many different colours as you like. To make the petals, pull off 8–10 small pieces of wool and tease them into a pointed or rounded petal shape. Felt these until they hold their shape, leaving the top end wispy to attach later. Tidy the edges of the petals with a single needle. If they seem a bit thin, you can always add a little more wool on top and felt them again. I sometimes like to add a different colour at the bottom like spots. Repeat to make all your petals.

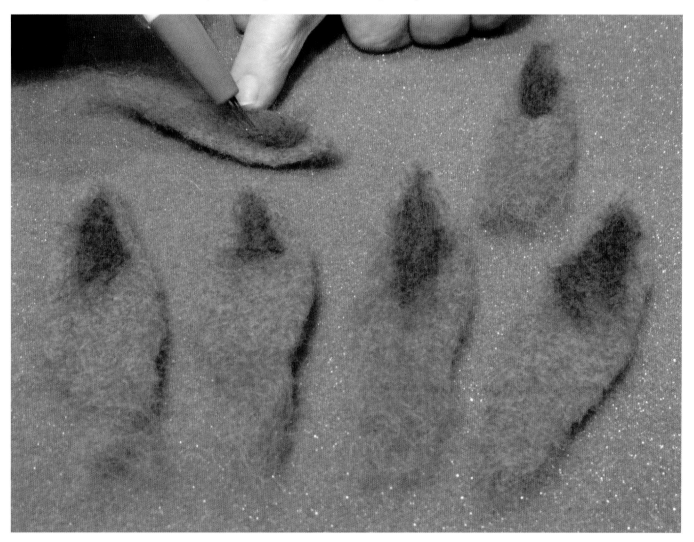

18. Now add the petals at the wispy ends by felting these into the body at the waist, overlapping them if you like or you can add a single layer and then add another layer of petals over the first layer. If your petals don't quite go around the body just simply make a few more and attach in the same way.

19. You can tie a pretty ribbon around her waist or make a sash or belt. To make a sash/belt, take a small strip of wool about 4cm (1.5in) wide and long enough to go around her waist plus a slight overlap (if you want ties then make it longer still). Felt the strip flat with a punch tool or multi needle and fold it widthways two or three times and felt it again; this gives it more body. Lay the band around the waist and felt to attach it, with the join at the front but just to the

side. Now felt around the top and the bottom edges just a little to attach it, or if you have made a longer sash, then tie it on. Cover the join with a pretty flower, which you can make by taking a tiny piece of wool, roll it into a ball in your fingers, felt it flat, add a centre in a contrasting colour and felt on to the band.

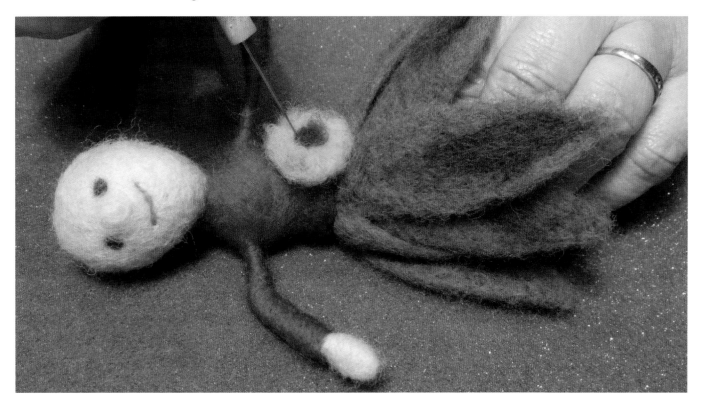

20. For the hair, you have a few options. You can use dyed or natural merino top or curly locks, either natural or dyed in your colour choice. It can be either short or long, you can leave it loose or tie it up. I will explain how to do both styles.

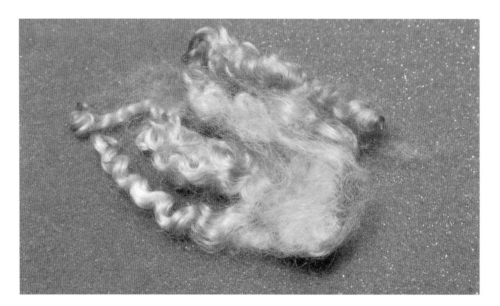

21. Using curls/locks. Take a small bunch of your chosen locks. When separating locks always pull them out of the bundle by the nice end, not the fuzzy end, to keep the nice pretty ends together in a curl as it came off the sheep. The fuzzy part is where it was shorn from the sheep and is the best end for felting into the head. Practise your hair style without felting to make sure you have enough hair. To attach shorter locks, I felt them into the head either side of the center parting. Leave them to hang down or to tie with a ribbon. If they are really long, you can felt the fuzzy ends deep into the head either in

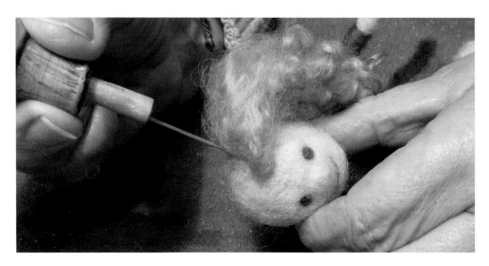

the middle of the head or to the side, taking care not to poke the needle out through the face. Then wrap the curls around the head until you get to the end of the curls and felt those ends down; this will give your fairy an updo style. You may find you have to felt it just up and away from the very end of the curl tips, as sometimes they can be tricky to felt down depending how thick they are. You should now have the head mainly covered, but you can add more curls in the same way anywhere if you need to. Push in your needle in a few places all over to help hold the hair on and in place. You can add some curls to hang down anywhere or you can leave it short. I quite like to add a little single bunch by felting them into the head, offset at the very top like a high ponytail. Your hairstyle will vary a bit as the length of the curls vary depending on the breed and even on the individual sheep. Nevertheless, whatever curls you use, felt

them into the head and then style them. Some of them can be very long so there may be enough length to be wrapped around and attached at the bottom of the head, and still leave some hanging down over the shoulder.

22. Using merino top: choose your colour of merino top. You will see that this is very different to the carded wool, as the staple length is a lot longer (the staple being the length of wool as it was on the sheep). To pull off a length of wool, take the end of the wool in one hand, hold the ball of wool in the other hand about 18cm (7in) away, and gently pull the wool apart. If it doesn't separate, move your hands slightly further apart until it does; the reason you cannot pull the wool off at a shorter length is that you cannot break the staple length without cutting it. When you have pulled a length off, split the length of wool into two thinner lengths. Decide where your parting is on the head and lay the length of hair on and with a 38 gauge single needle, just slightly down from that parting, felt along the middle of the piece of hair – folding the hair in half will

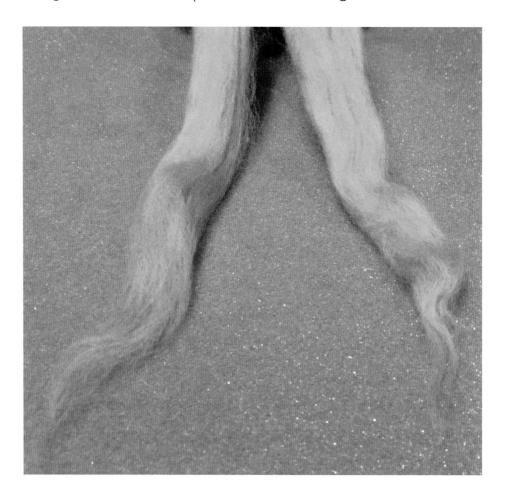

give you the middle. Now fold the top half down over the bottom piece of hair; this gives the hair a more natural look, rather than looking like it is stuck on. Repeat this on the other side of the head as close as possible to the first line. You can add another layer at the back if you feel it needs more hair, by repeating the process on the back of the head. Smooth the hair down with your hand gently, and carefully push the needle in through the hair in a few places to hold it in place. To add a little fringe at the front, take a tiny wisp of hair, bobble it up in your fingers and felt it at the very front of the

hairline. Style the hair how you want it – you could tie it, plait it or leave it loose, and you could trim it if you want a level finish. On mine, I pulled it to the side and felted to hold it in place.

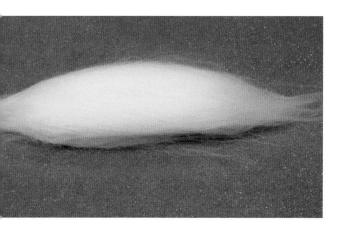

23. Now the wings! Take some white wool tops, pull a single staple length off, and lay it on your pad, then pull another layer so you have one on top of the other. Take another thin strand of white wool top and tie it around the middle as tightly as you can. Lay them back on your pad, fan the wings out and with your punch tool or multi needle, felt a small area on each wing close to the tie, which will help the wings stay fanned out nicely. This is optional; depending on the look you prefer, you can leave them not felted so they hang just as they are. Now attach the wings to the back of the fairy with a dab of glue, holding them down for a few minutes so they stick well.

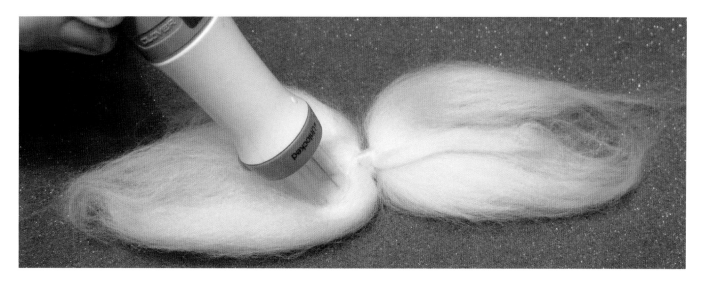

24. Finally, thread a piece of cord or ribbon on her so you can hang her up if you wish.

25. You could use this method in the same way to make a witch instead of a fairy simply by using dark colours like black, purple, green and orange. You can make a hat for a witch to go with this by following the hat instructions for the snowman or Christmas penguin in the other chapters.

Finished Standing Fairy.

Finished Fairy on Pumpkin.

Finished Fairy Bookends.

Finished Halloween Witch.

CHAPTER SIX

Cute Kitty

A cute, fluffy kitty in a colour of your choice, or based on your own furry friends!

For this project, you will need:

- Carded core wool batt
- Your choice of coloured carded wool batt for the body
- Black, white and pink carded wool batt
- Carded wool batt colour for the eyes
- Whiskers (horse hair or nylon thread)
- Ribbon
- 5 x 30cm (12in) pipe cleaners
- Wire cutters or sharp scissors

You need to firstly make two main shapes, one for the body and one for the head.

1. You will begin by making the body shape. Start by taking a piece of carded core wool, approximately 26cm x 16cm (10in x 6in), and lay this on your mat.

2. Next fold in the longer sides so they slightly overlap in the middle.

3. Now roll the wool up lengthways as tightly as you can, then felt the ends down to stop it from unrolling.

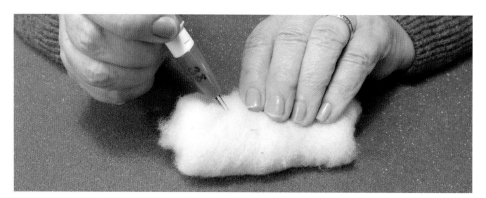

4. Start to needle felt the shape all over, working up and down the length and rolling it over as you go to make sure the whole body is being felted. Felt the base in from the end. Fold any loose wool at

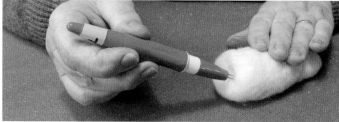

the top down and work this end into a rounded point.

5. Next wrap another layer of carded core wool around the whole body and felt the shape all over firmly. You should end up with a nice, firm body shape around 11cm high by 6cm wide (4in x 2in), with the bottom being fatter than the top. If you don't have the bottom fatter than the rest and need to make this larger, you can wrap more carded core wool just around the bottom area and felt this on to the desired size.

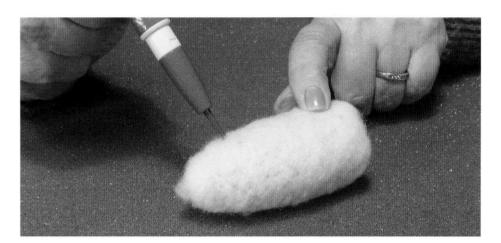

6. Now you will move on to the head shape. Take another piece of carded core wool, approximately 11cm x 8cms (4in x 3in), and fold it across widthways. Then roll this upwards into a sausage shape as tightly as you can, before felting it to stop it unrolling.

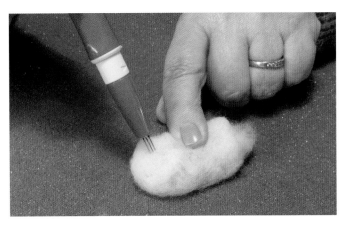 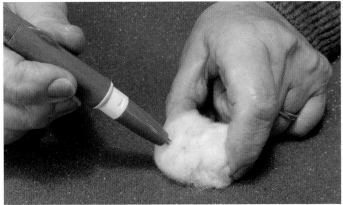

7. Next felt the shape all over, working towards creating an oval shape. If the oval is getting too long you can always fold the ends of it back towards the middle if you need to as you work at getting the shape right. Squeezing the shape with your fingers at the sides as you felt will help keep the shape.

8. Once you have an oval shape, if you think it is too small you can keep adding more thin layers of core wool by wrapping the shape and felting it each time. Try holding the head widthways on top of the previously made body to gauge the size you need to suit the body. When you are happy with the size, wrap a last final layer around the middle of the oval which will change it from an oval to more like a ball with flat sides.

9. Take a small piece of carded core wool, fold it and place this across the bottom half of the face, the face being one of the flat sides. Felt it until it is smooth; you should then have this shape.

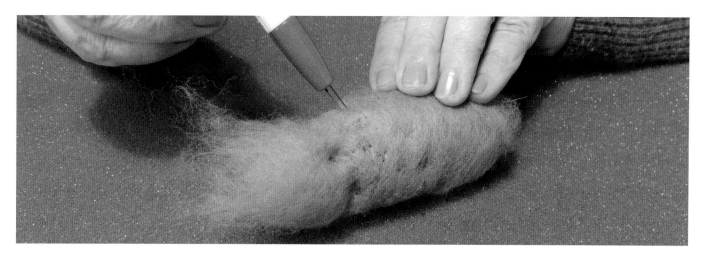

10. Now with your choice of coloured carded wool, pull off a strip of wool large enough to cover the body. Wrap this around the body and felt this on just enough to attach it, leaving the neck end wispy, as you will use this to attach the head.

11. Cover the head in the same way with your coloured wool. If you find any bare or thin places anywhere, you can patch them in by taking small wisps of wool and felting them on to these areas.

12. Now it is time to start adding the cat's features. Add an extra piece of wool on the bottom half of the face and felt it smooth to create the muzzle area. It needs to be a reasonably solid raised area as you will felt features into it so keep adding wool until you have enough.

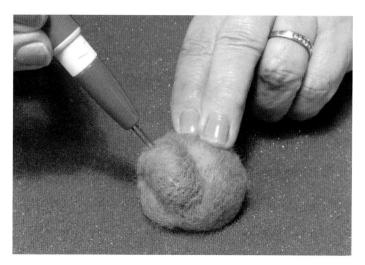

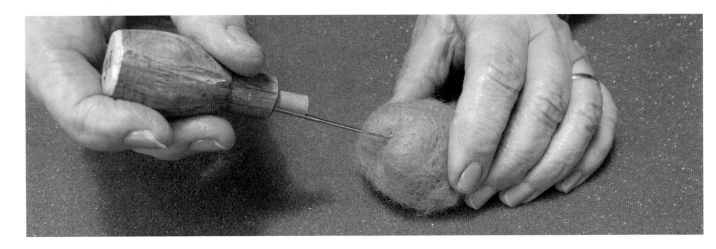

13. Now needle felt a line into it, down the middle to define the muzzle area.

14. Next, taking a small piece of pink wool, fold this into a tiny triangle shape and carefully place it (straight side at the top) on to the middle of the muzzle, then felting it on around the outside only, leaving the middle to stand out.

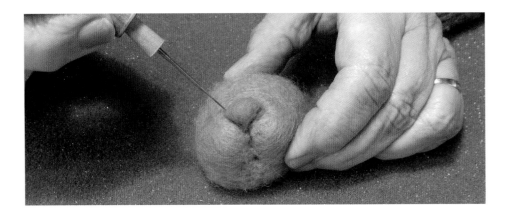

15. Now take a very small wisp of pink (or you could use black or brown if preferred) and roll this between your fingers to make a thread. Felt this on to the muzzle below the nose into a 'V' shape to form the cat's mouth.

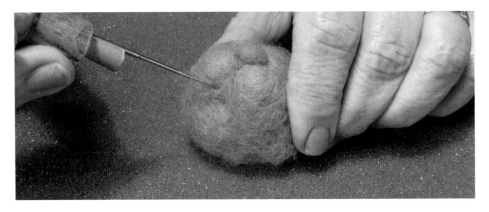

16. Now you can work on the eyes, and there are two options here:

a. Option 1 – felted eyes! Using a coarse single needle, mark where the eyes will be on the face – they sit level with the top of the nose and quite close together. On these marks felt a slight indentation, so when you add the eyes they don't sit proud from the rest of the face. Choose your colour eyes – I like to blend a main colour with hints of another, for example green eyes with hints of brown or yellow or both. Take a wisp of your chosen main eye colour large enough for both eyes, and if wishing to blend more colours in, do this by adding a little of the alternative colour(s) on top. Then, carefully pulling the wool apart and restacking, repeat this step until the colours are mixed together well. Take a small piece of this and felt this on to the indentations in an oval shape. Once the main eye colour is on, take a small piece of black wool and felt this into the middle of each eye to form the pupil, felting these just enough to hold them in place. Now, take a very tiny wisp of white wool and rub this between your fingers to form it into a tiny ball, and then felt this on to the eyes for light reflection. You can then carefully line the eyes in a dark colour by taking a wisp of wool, rubbing this into a thread, and felt around the outside of the eyes – this step is to suit your own preference, I think some colours of cat suit this addition and some don't.

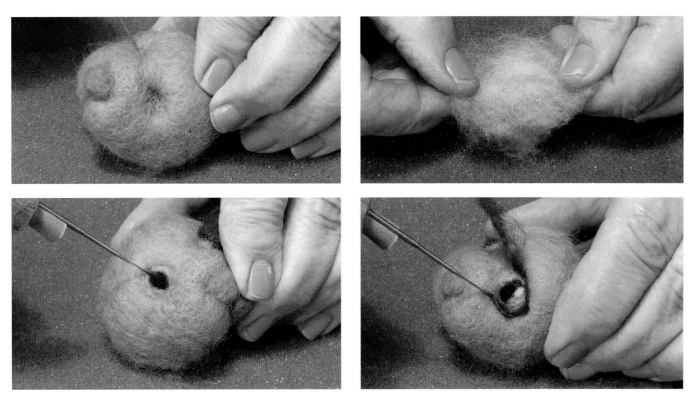

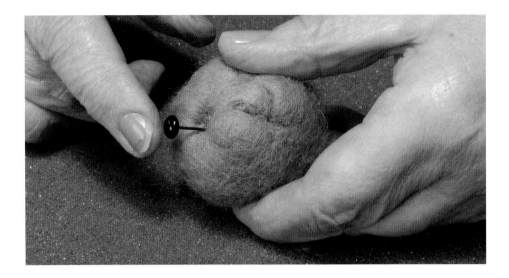

b. Option 2 – glass eyes! You can get glass cats' eyes in various colours and sizes, or there are plain black eyes. These normally have some form of stalk on the back in varying forms. To set these into the head, firstly make indentations where the eyes will be as you would for felted eyes. Next push a sharp awl into the indentations to make a hole deep enough for the stalk, and check this before going on to the next part. Once your holes are deep enough, add a little glue to the end of the stalks and push them into place. Once the glass eyes are in, you can take small wisps of wool in your face colour and felt them in around the outside of your eye to cover any slight gaps or joins.

17. Now you can join the head to the body. To do this, place the head upside down on your pad and hold the body on top; make sure the back of the head and back of the body sit roughly in line with each other, then felt the loose wool from the body into the head, working it in all the way around. Once it is firmly attached, cover the join by adding wisps of wool in your body colour and lay them over the join vertically and felt on smoothly with no folds.

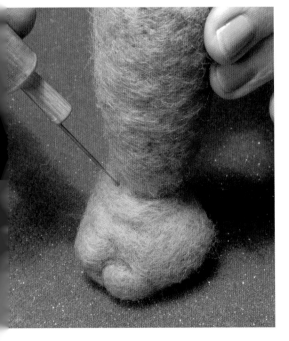

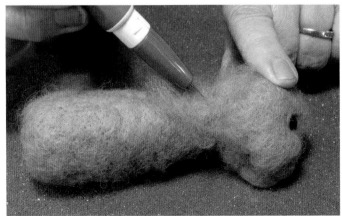

18. Before you make the legs, check you are happy with the shape of your cat. You could make it a bit fatter if you wish by adding another layer of your cat's body colour wool on to the body where you want to build it up, or you may prefer a slim cat. This is where you make the creation your own.

19. Now to make the front legs. Take a 30cm (12in) pipe cleaner and fold in half, then twist it together – this makes it a bit sturdier. Take one leg and on the folded over end bend a paw. To check this is the right length, hold it against the body with the paw level with the bottom of your cat and check where it will attach to the body at shoulder level. If the leg is too long and needs shortening just fold over any excess, this way if you need to alter it you still have the wire there.

20. Now pull off a long thin strip of carded core wool, then wrap it around the pipe cleaner in a single wrap as tightly as you can. Make sure you keep the wool flat as you wrap, and don't let it twist. Usually one layer will be enough but it will depend a bit on how thick you want your legs, so this is up to you to decide. If you find the wool

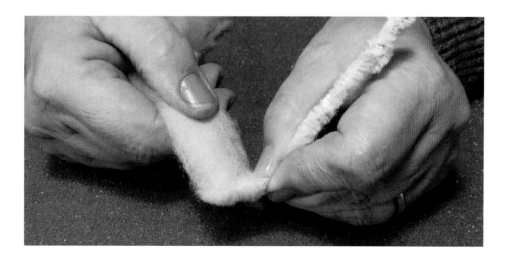

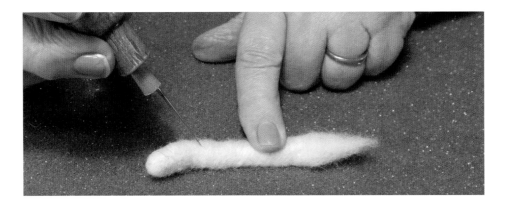

is too short don't panic, just felt the end of the wool to ensure it doesn't unroll, and then add another strip to finish the leg; if there is too much wool, just pull off any excess. When it is wrapped, with a single needle felt very carefully to avoid the wire. The best way is to insert your needle so hopefully it skims over, under and beside the wire. Felt until this is nice and firm, leaving a little loose wool at the top for attaching to the body.

21. Next add some extra wool around the paw to make it a little larger.

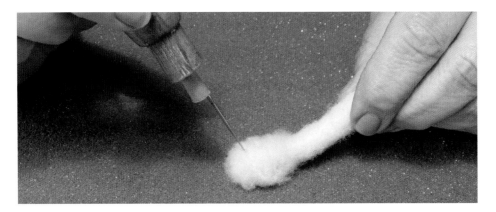

22. Repeat steps 20 and 21 to complete other front leg.

23. Now to make the back legs. Using 30cm (12in) pipe cleaners, bend each one in half and twist them together as you did with the front legs. Fold out about 2.5cm (2in) for the foot and turn the rest upwards. Wrap the foot of the back leg in the same way as the front legs, remembering to keep it tight when wrapping and make it a little thicker for the paws as you did with the front legs.

24. Now wrap some extra wool around the wire at the top, which will be the thigh and what you use to attach it to the body.

25. Repeat steps 23 and 24 to make the other back leg.

26. Now cover all four of the legs with your coloured topcoat wool and felt them smooth.

27. You can now add the legs to the body. Sit the body upright and place one of the back legs against it to decide where to position these. The body should sit flat on the surface and then position the leg towards the back. Laying the body flat on your pad, felt the wool around the top of the leg into the body until it is secure. Repeat with the other back leg. Make sure they are level by sitting it upright and checking it.

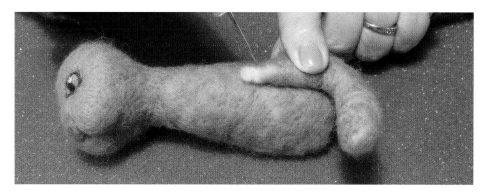

28. Next take a piece of wool and fold it into a pad shape. Lay this over the top of where the thigh attaches to the body and felt this on into a rounded shape. Felt it all over but leave it a bit puffy on the thigh. Repeat with the other back leg.

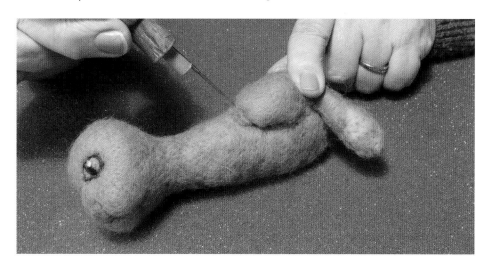

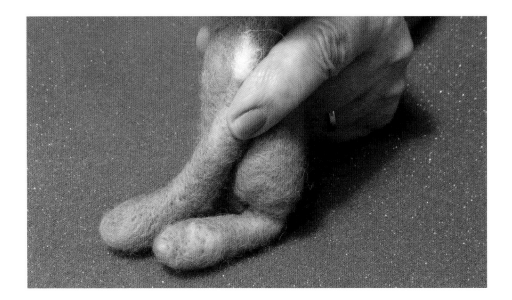

29. Now let us attach the front legs. Sit your cat upright and hold a front leg against it to see where it comes to; ideally you want to attach it at about shoulder height. If you need to adjust the legs, you can add length by unfolding the top of the pipe cleaner or shorten them by snipping off any excess pipe cleaner. Lay your cat on the pad and felt the front leg on both sides of the wire into the body. Felt it on so it is firm and it holds the cat sitting up and stable. Repeat with the other front leg.

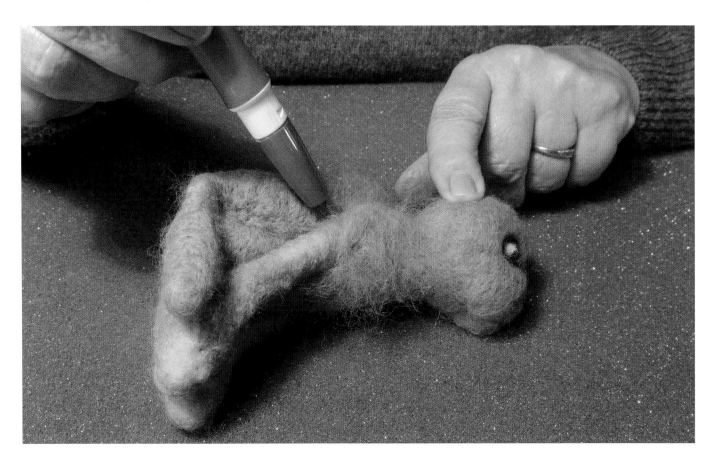

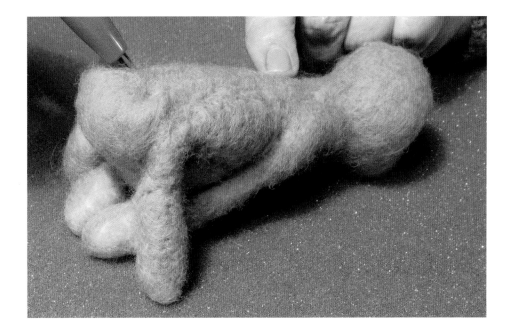

30. Now you can add small wisps of wool all over the cat, building up any areas that may need it and covering to hide up any joins, particularly where the legs are attached. If your cat tips back when it is sitting, you can felt a bit of wool on the bottom to level him up, but remember to cover any joins.

31. At this point you can also add a cute, white chest to your cat by felting on wisps of white wool between his front legs. You can also add wisps of white on his paws if wanted.

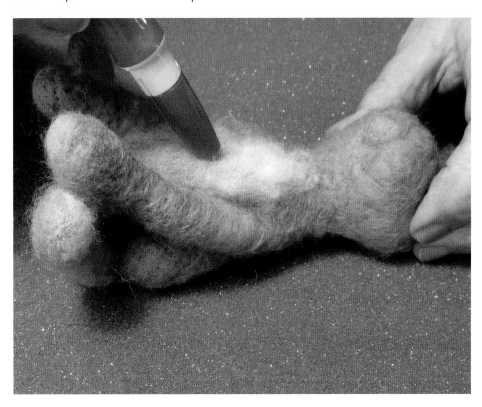

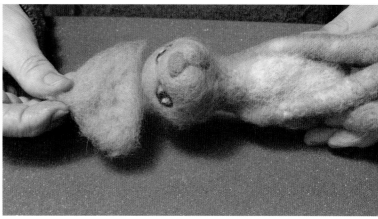

32. Now you can make some ears. Pull off some wool and on your mat lay out two pieces folded into triangles as near to the same size as you can get them. The base of the triangle needs to be quite wide; each triangle base should be only a bit smaller than the width of the head. Felt them flat on the pad to form the ears, you can use your punch or multi tool here to speed this process up. Remember to lift them off sometimes so they don't get stuck to the pad! To form the sides and the top points of the ears, fold just the very edges in so you get a nice firm edge on the ears. If the edges are thin and need thickening up, fold some wisps around the sides and felt them again. You should end up with two very similar well-felted ears.

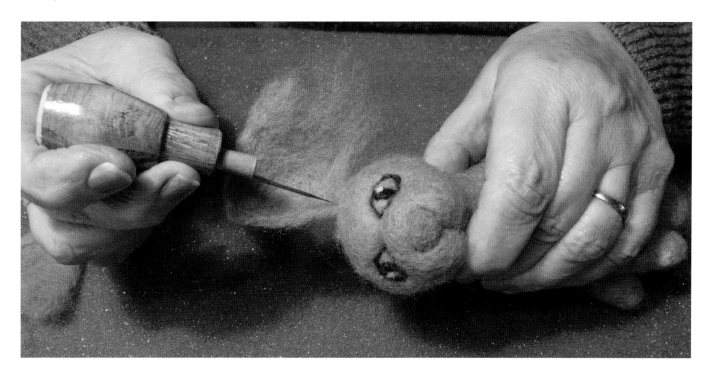

33. To attach these, take the first ear, place it on the top of the head towards the back and felt the inside corner on first to attach it. Cats' ears don't meet in the middle so make sure there is a gap between them. Gradually bend the ear around and attach the other corner to the outside of the head. If you are happy with the position then work your way around the ear base to attach it to the head completely. If you are not quite happy when you have secured both corners, you can carefully pull it off and re-attach it in a new position. Repeat this process with the other ear.

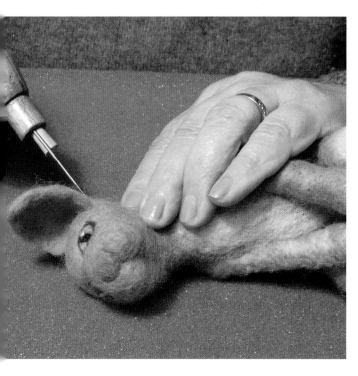

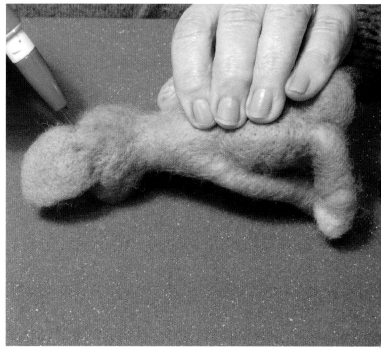

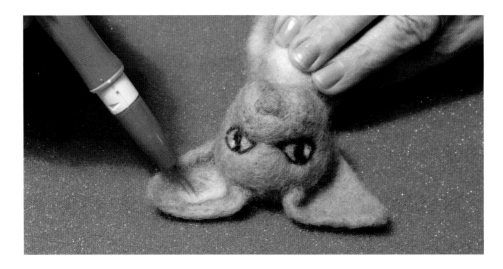

34. Once both ears are attached, felt a little wool over the joins. You can also add some wisps of pink or white inside the ear if you wish.

35. Now the tail. Fold another 30cm (12in) pipe cleaner in half and really nip the bend up with pliers so it has a good point on it as this will be the tail's tip. Twist the pipe cleaner together. Taking strips of carded core wool, tightly wrap the tail; it doesn't really matter which end you start, but here you will start at the base of the tail. The easiest way is to hold the wool on between your thumb and index finger and turn the pipe cleaner, not the wool, working your way down towards the tip, felting it as you go. The base of the tail should be a bit thicker than the tip, so if needed, add another thin wisp at the tail base, gradually letting it get thinner as it goes up.

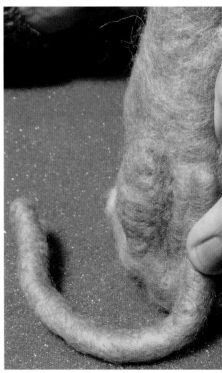

36. Once you are happy with the shape, cover the tail with your coloured wool, carefully felting this on until it is nice and firm.

37. Hold the tail on the cat and decide on the length. If you think the tail is too long, simply cut off the excess at the base, not the tip!

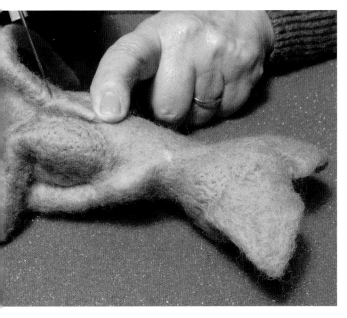 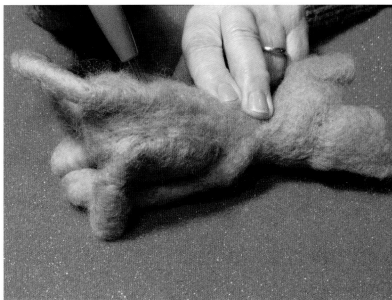

38. To attach the tail, lay the base of the tail on the cat. Carefully felt the tail on by felting the loose wool into the body around both sides of the wire. Once it is firmly attached, you can then cover the joins with more wisps of wool.

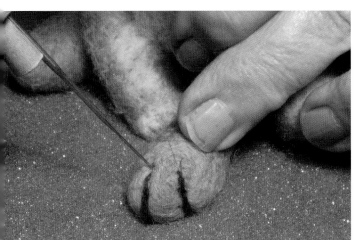 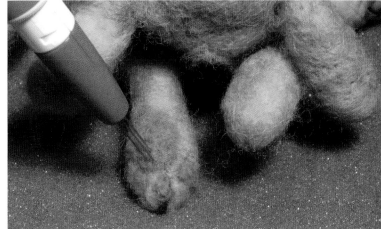

39. To add lines to the paws for the toes, take some small pieces of wool, twist them into threads and felt short lines on the front of the paws. You could also felt some cute little pink pads on the bottom of the feet!

40. To finish off your cute kitty, look at your cat from all angles – if you want to cover any joints or build an area up to make him fatter then just add more small wispy pieces of wool, a little at a time, until you are happy with it. I usually do quite a bit of adding wool at this stage, often building up his bum, tummy or where the legs join; this is where you make the cat your unique project. If you wanted, you could add some markings such as stripes or patches.

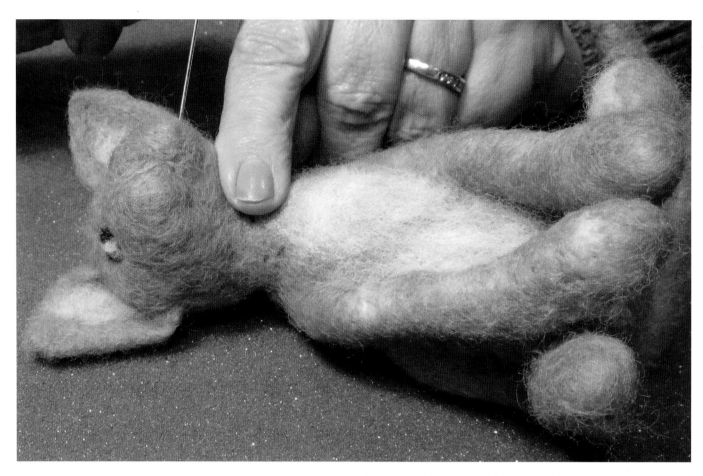

41. One last personal choice option is whiskers. I use horse mane or tail hair, but if you are not able to source this, you could use very thin nylon thread or long bristles from a soft brush. Depending on how long they are you can thread them through with a sewing needle so that one whisker does both sides, adding a tiny bit of glue to stop them pulling right through. Alternatively, if they are short whiskers you can make tiny holes with your awl or felting needle, pop a little bit of glue on the end of your whisker and push the end in the holes.

Finished Kitty
with Ball of Wool.

CHAPTER SEVEN

Wet Felted Picture

This lovely picture is made by using a wet felted background, enhanced with needle felted details.

To make this picture, you will need:
- Natural wool batting for the base
- Carded wool batts in various shades of green and blue, or just a single shade of each will do
- Various colours of wool batting and wool tops for the flowers, leaves etc.
- A towel
- A piece of bubble wrap and a piece of plain plastic, both a bit larger than your piece of batting
- A piece of netting or voile (an old piece of net curtain is ideal) large enough to cover the batting square
- A sprinkler or sponge
- A bamboo mat or something to roll with (a pool noodle or a piece of foam pipe insulation or a piece of wooden doweling, a rolling pin or a rolled up towel will do)
- Soap (olive oil is best)
- Dishwashing liquid
- Jug of warm water
- Needle felting pad
- Single needle
- Multi tool

PART 1 – WET FELTED BACKGROUND

1. On a table or work surface, lay out your towel. On top of this lay your bubble wrap, bubbles facing upwards.

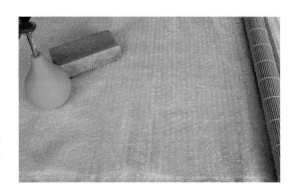

Finished Felted Picture.

2. Tear off a square of your natural batting approximately 23cm x 23cm (9in x 9in). If it is too thick you may need to split its thickness in half. If it is uneven, you can pull pieces off and patch it to get the square even. Lay this square on top of your bubble wrap.

3. Start at the top to make the sky. Pull off strips of your blue wool and lay them down on top of the square, slightly overlapping each time. If using multiple shades, start with the darkest, graduating the shades as you work down the square. Continue laying blue strips to around halfway down the square. Keep to a single layer of wool for now; you can patch up any thin areas later. Sometimes a wisp of

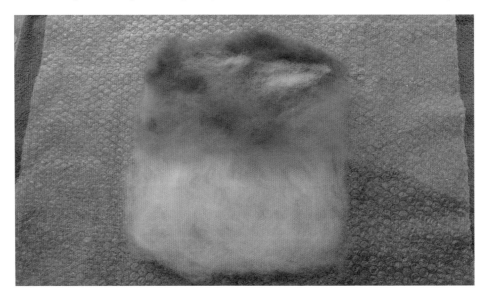

purple or pink can look pretty in the sky, and a faint wisp of white if you want a cloud or two.

4. Now do the same using the green wool for the grass. Overlap your strips of green as you work from the bottom up to meet the sky. When you meet the sky, lay the green slightly over the blue where they meet, and then try to arrange where they meet so it isn't in a perfectly straight line.

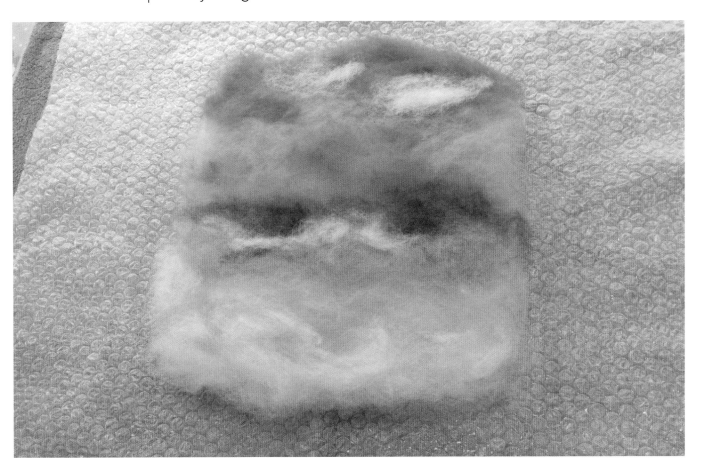

5. Now look at your picture and find any thin areas that may need patching. To patch these in, pull off thin pieces of wool and lay them over these areas. You want there to be just enough cover to ensure the natural wool square base doesn't show through, but you don't want it to be too thick either as it will take a lot longer to felt.

6. Feel your work all over with your hands flat to make sure it is reasonably smooth and even. Now is your final chance to add any extra wisps of colour before the piece is wetted up.

7. On top of your picture, very carefully lay your piece of netting. Try to get it placed correctly the first time, as if you lift it up you risk the wool catching on it and lifting out of the layout you have just created.

8. Add a splash of soap to your warm water. Carefully wet the picture all over with your sprinkler or sponge.

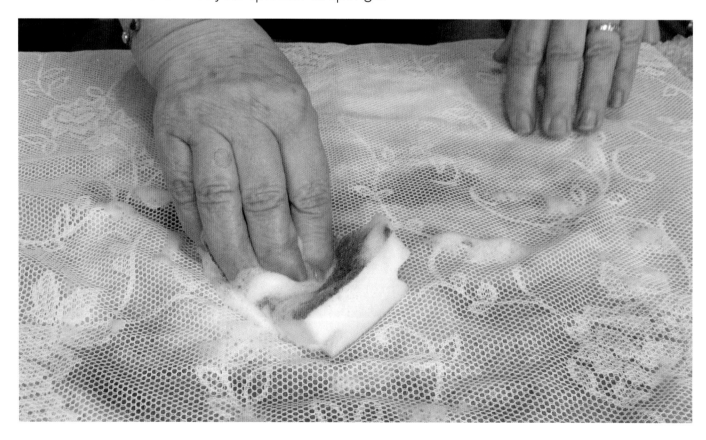

9. Then, using your hands or a sponge, add a little more soap all over. Press the soap and water into the wool, pushing the air out. If when you press down there are areas of your picture that are raised, this means there is still air underneath, so the picture needs more wetting down in that area.

10. Once it is thoroughly wet and the air has been pushed out, add a bit more soap using your hands (or rubbing with a soap bar) over your work.

11. Now very lightly slide your hands in a circular motion over the surface of your work. Your hands should glide over easily; if they don't then you possibly haven't got enough soap on the piece. You don't want too much soap, but there should be enough that when you run your hand across, you can see a trail of soap. Your piece should be thoroughly wet all the way through but not swimming in water. If you think you have too much water, then blot it out by pressing a spare towel on top of the netting.

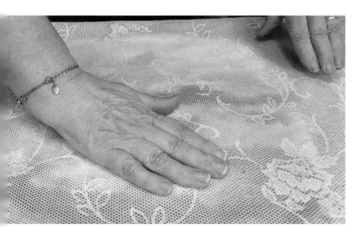

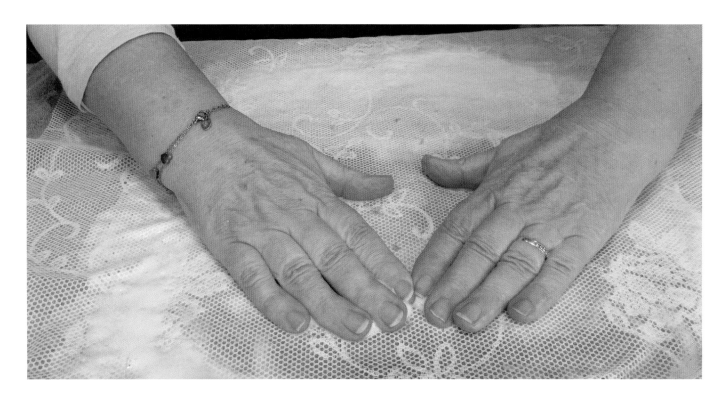

12. Carry on lightly rubbing the work (but not pressing hard on it) for approximately 15–20 minutes in circles, side to side and up and down. Carefully lift your netting every five minutes to check it isn't sticking to your wool; if it is you may be rubbing a bit too hard. If it sticks, lay one hand on the wool to hold it down and gently peel back the netting. If you find your work keeps sticking to the netting, you can swap the netting for your sheet of plastic, adding water and soap on top of this to making the rubbing easier. All this work is forming a skin on your piece of felt, so that when you get to rolling your wool it all stays in place.

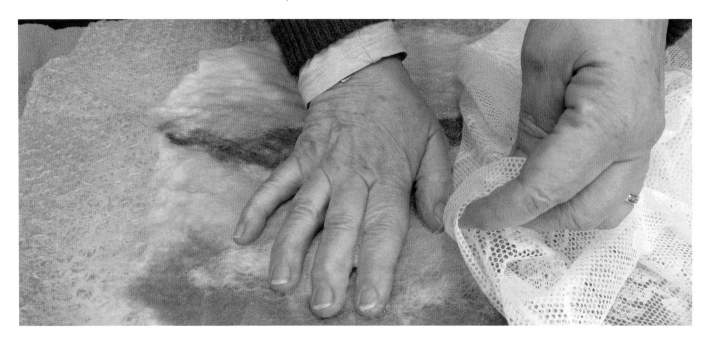

13. Once you have finished the rubbing process, peel off the netting and test your picture to see if it is starting to felt by pinching up a small piece of wool (the pinch test). If it seems the wool is loose and you could still pull wool off, then you need to put your net back on and carry on rubbing for a bit longer. If it seems that it is holding together and you would not be able to pull wool off, then it is felted enough to move to the next stage. Remove the netting and replace this with the sheet of plastic making sure it is still wet and soapy, adding more water and soap if you need too. You can tidy your edges at any point when you are checking your work by pushing any stray wool back with your fingers.

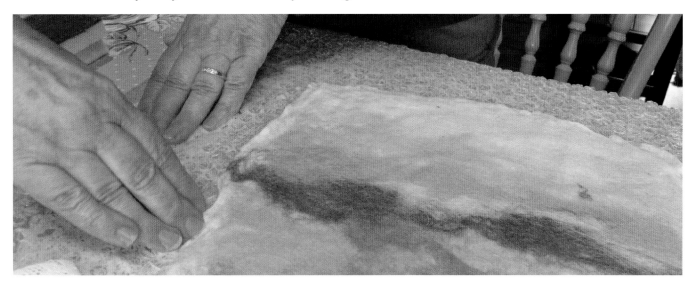

14. To carry on felting your work you now need to roll it; this is where your felt will shrink down and firm up. Lay the towel on the table first and if you have a bamboo mat, lay this flat out on top of the towel followed by your piece of felt, still in the bubble wrap and plastic. Then roll the three parts up together as tightly as you can (towel, bamboo mat and your work). If you are using a pool noodle or similar, lay your towel down with your felt wrapped in the plastic on top, then lay your roller on top of your work at the very bottom and roll these all up together as tight as you can.

15. Now put your hands firmly on top of the towel and roll it backwards and forwards fifty times. If at any time the roll becomes loose, stop and rewrap it tightly. The tighter it is wrapped, the better it will hold when you are rolling.

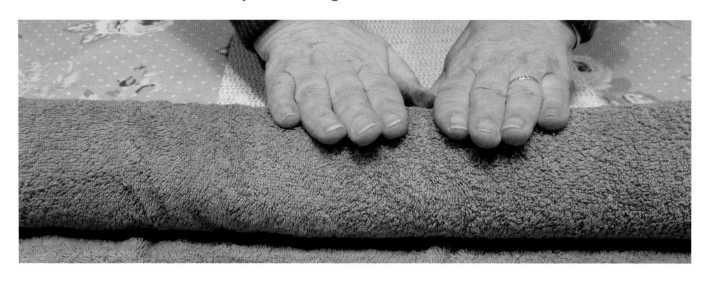

16. After the fifty rolls, unwrap the plastic package from the towel, unroll the bubble wrap and the plastic but don't remove it from your felt. Pick your felt/plastic layer up and rotate this 90 degrees clockwise. Wrap your work back up again in the same way and repeat another fifty rolls.

17. Repeat the unrolling, rotating the felt 90 degrees clockwise, re-rolling up then rolling fifty times, two more entire times. You should then have rolled it from all four sides and done 200 rolls in total.

18. When you have rolled from all four sides and are back where you started, unroll everything, but leaving the felt in the plastic, lift your felt up and turn it the other way up, so you have the reverse of the picture on top.

19. Now wrap it up again in the same way and roll fifty times, again rotating clockwise after each fifty rolls, repeating four times to take your back to where you started again, with all four sides having another fifty rolls completed. By this point, you should have done 400 rolls of the work, 200 face down, and then 200 face up.

20. Next unroll your felt and remove the top layer of plastic. Check your felt to see if it has felted. At this stage, it should be a nice, firm piece of felt. If you think it isn't quite there yet, then carry on with the rolling for a bit longer. I would suggest another 5–10 rolls each way should do it.

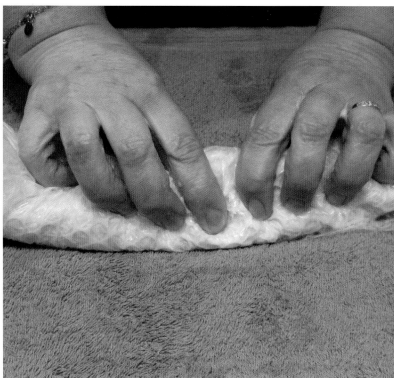

21. Now remove the sheet of plastic and if it feels a little dry and there's not much soap left, add a little more soap and warm water to your piece of felt. Now give your felt a good rub on both sides. To 'full' your felt do a combination of these things: rub it against itself a bit, roll it up just in the bubble wrap and roll it a few times equally from each way, bundle it up and throw it down hard on to your surface a few times. Now give it a good stretch back into shape. Doing all these things will turn it into a nice firm piece of felt for you to needle felt your picture on to.

22. Now, thoroughly rinse all the soap out of your felt. If you have any white vinegar, you could add a very tiny splash to some lukewarm water and let it sit in that for 10–15 minutes to restore the pH to the wool. Not everyone does this, so if you don't have any, not to worry. Remove your felt from the water and squeeze excess water out. Stretch your felt back into shape and leave laid flat out somewhere to dry before you add your needle felted design. The edges won't be dead straight, this is what is so lovely about it; each piece is unique.

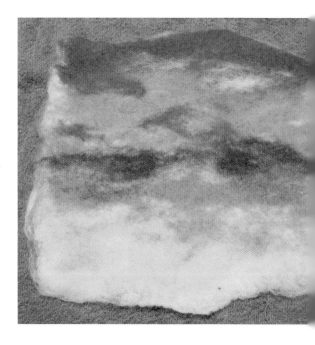

PART 2 – NEEDLE FELTED PICTURE

23. You can design your picture in your own unique way, so I will show you how to needle felt some different flowers, stalks, leaves, toadstools and birds on to your piece of felt. You can then use these techniques to place them in your picture wherever you want, and I am sure once you have got going you will come up with other ideas of your own! Gather all your colours together, greens, greys, browns and yellows for the foliage and any carded wool and merino top colours you have for your flowers. Use a single needle for the stalks, and anything else that needs to be in a thin line and controlled, and a multi tool for thicker leaves.

24. Start by taking a piece of green wool in a strip and placing on to your picture for a stalk. Start by felting the very end of the strip into your picture. Gradually draft (pull) the wool upwards, felting it into your felt background in a line, steering it into the direction you want the stalk to go.

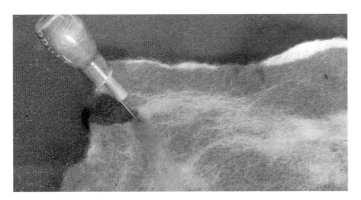 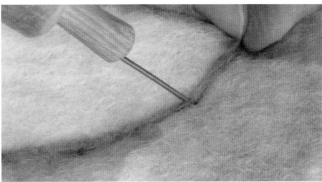

25. Repeat to add more stalks of different length, colour and shades of green or brown to get you started, you can always add more later.

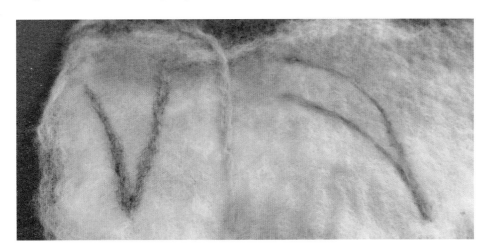

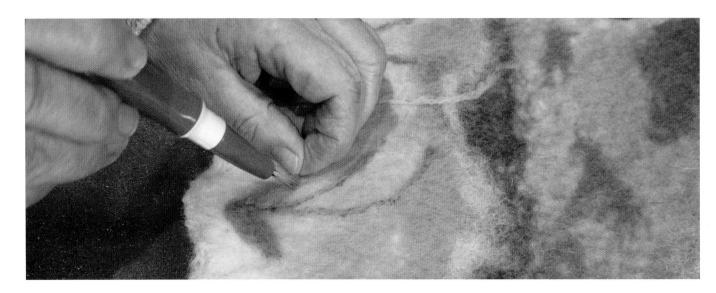

26. To add some leaves to the stalks, pull off small tufts of your chosen colour and fold them into a tiny leaf shapes with your fingers. Place these on the stalk and carefully felt them in. Vary the size and colours of your leaves for each stalk if you want to. To add very thin leaves you can also draft them on to the stalk in the same way you made the stalk itself. Varying the thickness of the wool will change the results you get, adding textures to your work. You could also add a little yellow or other shades of green on the edges of the leaves.

27. You can add a tree to your picture in the same way. Take a strip of your brown wool, the thickness being dependent on the size of tree you want, and placing the bottom of the tree at the base of your picture, draft the wool upwards using your needle to felt it in as you go. You can add branches, drafting the wool in the same way, or if they are short branches, just take small pieces of wool, twist them between your fingers and felt them on. Use your needle to felt on wisps of colour for leaves, blossom or fruit. You could add different

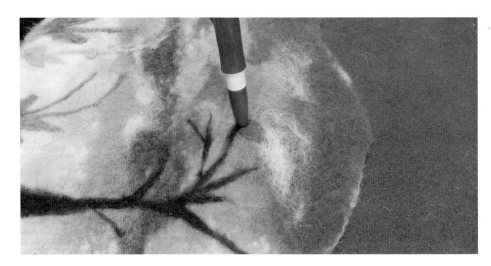

shades of brown on to the tree trunk and branches for shading too.

28. Birds can be added by twisting tiny wisps of black or brown and using your needle to felt them in. Clouds can be added by taking wisps of white wool and felting them into the picture, shaping them as you felt.

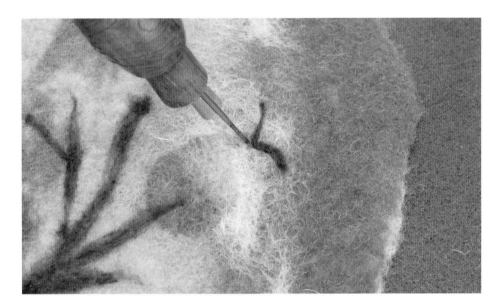

29. Now to add the flowers. To make a tall flower, like a foxglove on a tall stalk for example, take tiny pieces of purple wool, ball them up in your fingers and felt on to the top of your stalk. Repeat to add a cluster of balls to the top of the stalk, continuing to work down the stalk, gradually making them larger as you go.

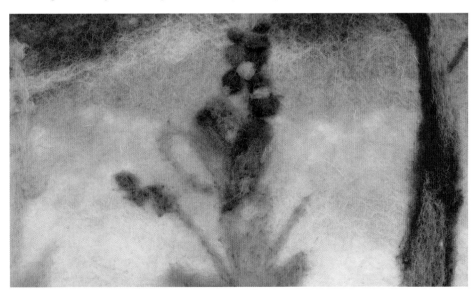

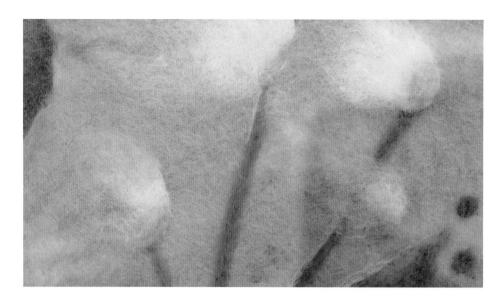

30. To make a dandelion-type flower, take a pinch of white and felt it into the background leaving one side loose. On the other side, felt in a wisp of pale yellow and add a touch of gold or orange as well.

31. For the flowers with petals, you can use a plain colour of wool or you can blend two colours together. To blend, stack wisps of colour on top of each other and pull apart, restacking and repeating this until the colours are mixed up. Take a wisp of the wool and fold it in half, place it where you want it with the folded end being the top of the petal and the wispy ends where it meets in the centre of the flower, then felt it on to the picture. You could also place the petal on the picture the other way so that you get a different shape of petal. I usually add an uneven number of petals, you can put on however many you want. Now add a wisp of another colour for the centre. You can also lay the petals in a half circle with no centre, to make this look like the same flower from another angle.

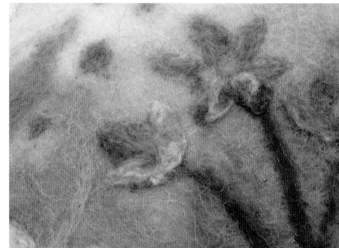

32. Take wisps of any colours, roll into balls and felt on to the picture on the grass in clusters to add flowers on the ground scattered here and there.

33. To make the rose-like flower, I use merino tops. Take a short strand and curl it into a circle with your fingers before carefully laying it on to your picture and felting it in the centre to attach. Try to catch in the ends while you felt it on and then carefully felt in a few places around the outside to help fix it in securely. You can then add a pretty colour for the centre.

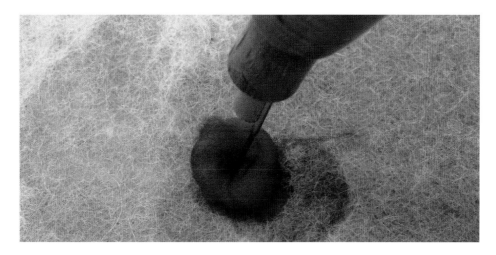

34. Now you can needle felt away and fill your picture with all you have learnt, in your own design and layout, and I am sure that you will be able to come up with your own flower ideas, add a sun, a rainbow, a cottage … felt away!

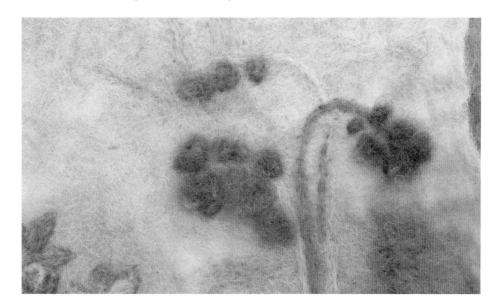

CHAPTER EIGHT

Seasonal Projects

SPRING – EASTER BUNNY

Make this cute bunny into a brooch, key ring, magnet or hanging decoration.

Finished Easter Bunny.

You will need:

- Carded core wool batt
- Carded wool batt in your colour of choice
- Whiskers (optional)
- Brooch back, key ring, magnet or string

1. Take a piece of core wool about 18cm x 10cm (7in x 4in) and fold it up lengthways 5cm (2in) each time, then fold it the opposite way

into three. Holding it tightly, felt it all over, starting with the join so it doesn't unroll. Felt it all over and around the sides to form a thick disc of wool just under 5cm (2in) diameter and 2cm (¾in) deep. This is the face.

2. Take another small piece of core wool and fold into a ball a bit smaller than the disc. Hold this on top of your disc and felt around the outside to attach it to the face first, to create the nose. Now shape this dome by felting it all over to form the head shape, working towards having a point for the nose that sits towards the bottom of the face, rather than in the middle. You can then add more wool to build the nose area up if you don't think it is quite large enough. About 4cm (1.5in) depth from the point of the nose to the back is about right.

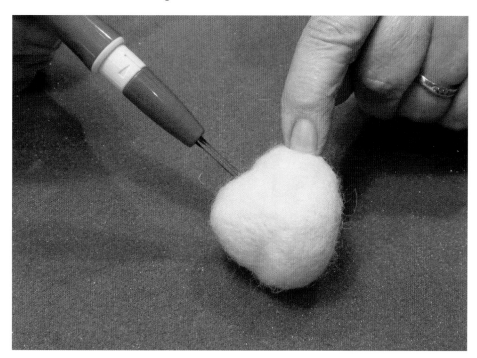

3. Cover the whole head with a layer of your chosen topcoat colour and felt it on. You can do this in two stages by covering the front first, wrapping and felting the wool around the edges, and then covering the back and any missed areas.

4. Place your bunny head on your pad the right way up to add the nose. Take a tiny piece of pink wool, fold it into a triangle and with the point of the triangle facing downwards, attach the nose on to the point by holding it on and felting along the top line first and then down the sides.

5. Next, take another tiny wisp of pink wool, roll it in your fingers to make a thread, place on the head below the nose in a rounded W-shape, and felt on as you go to create the bunny's mouth.

6. Using a coarse needle, something like a 36 or 38, firmly felt two indentations, equal in size, somewhere around the middle line of the head and

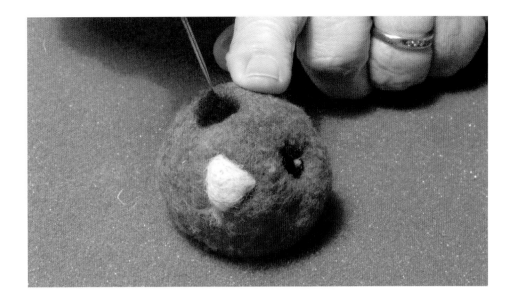

either side of the nose, to form the eyes. Now take tiny wisps of black wool and felt these into the indentations. You could also add a dot of white wool in the eye, if you want to, by felting this on to the black eye.

7. For the ears, lay out two equal pieces of your topcoat wool on to your pad and mould them into an ear shape. Using your punch/multi tool, felt them a few times down the middle of the ear, leaving them wispy at the bottom for attaching to the head, then shape them at the edges by folding the wool over slightly to get a smooth edge. You can then add a little white or pink in the middle of your ear, being careful not to felt right through the ears, as you will push

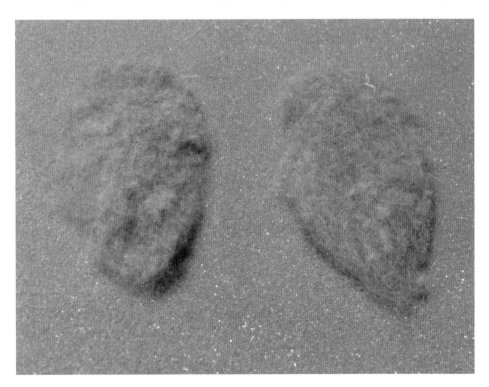

the new colour out the other side. If this does happen, just snip the pink wool off at the back of the ears with scissors.

8. Attach the ears to the head in the position you want them, I placed mine toward the outside of the bunny head, but you can have them closer together if you prefer, or even hanging downwards. Hold the ears in place and with a single 38 needle felt the wispy ends into the head from the front and the back until they are attached securely. Take tiny wisps of your topcoat wool and felt them over the joins on both the front and back of the ears.

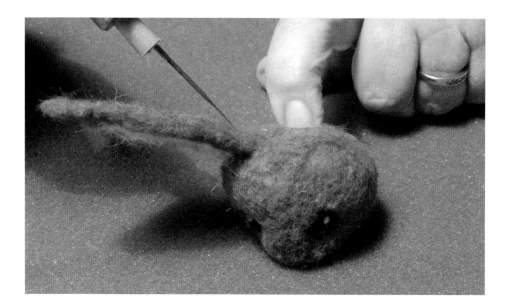

9. Add two little balls of wool either side of the nose by felting in, in either your topcoat colour or you could use white wool.

10. Now to finish the head off, you can add a final fine wispy layer of wool, very lightly felted in all over to give your bunny a fluffy appearance or you can leave it smooth if you prefer.

11. You could add some whiskers by threading them through with a sewing needle from one side to the other, adding a tiny dab of glue and then pulling the glue inside the head. Trim the whiskers with scissors.

12. Now you can add what you need to make your bunny into whatever you want! To make a brooch, flatten the back a little by felting it several times before sewing or glueing on the brooch back, then covering the bar with a little wool. You could instead add a key ring chain, glue on a magnet or simply sew on a ribbon to hang as a decoration for Easter.

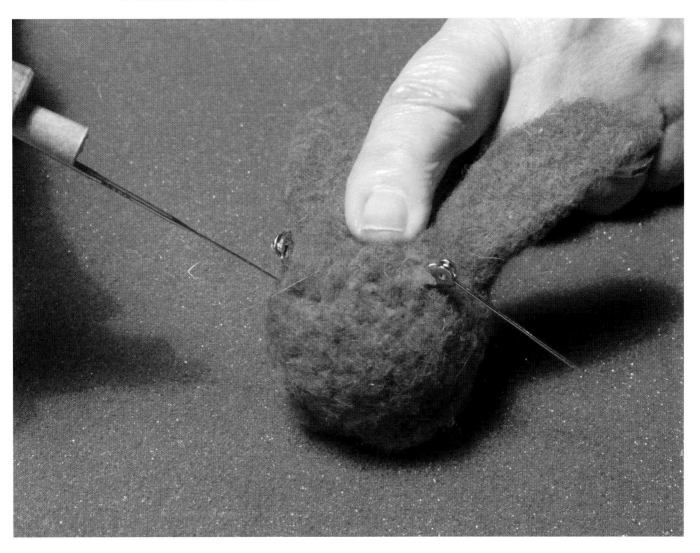

Finished Easter Egg Basket.

SPRING – COLOURED FELT EASTER EGGS

Don't be fooled into thinking this is an easy project! It can take some time and patience to produce a nice smooth well-shaped egg.

You will need:

- Carded wool batt in a variety of colours

1. As these are small, I don't worry about using a core wool to make them so start by pulling off a handful of your chosen colour wool. Find a way to work out the amount of wool you use, so you can make sure all the eggs you make are the same size, or as near as you can anyway! You could measure it by feel in your hand, or you can weigh it if you want to – micro scales are ideal for weighing these tiny amounts. I usually use a piece about 15cm x 7cm (6in x 3in).

2. Fold your wool in half lengthways first, then fold it in half widthways, and then roll it up as tight as you possibly can. Felt the loose ends so it doesn't unroll.

 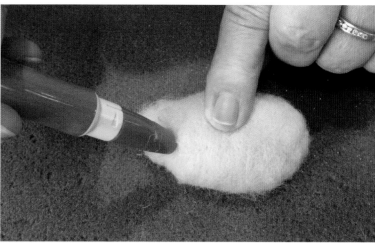

3. Now work on the ends of the egg. If one end looks fatter than the other, then use that for the larger, bottom end of the egg ... if not just choose an end. Felt into the end diagonally, so you are pushing the wool from the end into the centre of the egg; this will stop the egg from getting too long. Once this end is starting to form, turn the egg around and work in the same diagonal stance, focusing on making this the pointed end of the egg.

4. When you have the two ends formed, work your way all over the egg, gradually firming it up and felting it all over. Now you can add a thin layer completely over the whole egg and felt it with a fine needle, to get a nice smooth finish. If you want larger eggs then you can simply wrap thin layers over it until you have the desired size, and felt until smooth. If you have a Clover punch tool, you can use it all over the egg and this will give you an extra-smooth finish.

5. You could also add patterns to the egg. Add little dots or flowers by carefully needle felting the colour you want on to it.

6. Similar things to the previous bunny project can be made with the eggs: a brooch, magnet, key ring or perhaps hang it with some thread for a decoration on an Easter tree. I love having several different-coloured plain pastel shades of egg in a little Easter basket; I think they look so pretty!

Finished Halloween Pumpkin.

AUTUMN – HALLOWEEN PUMPKINS

Lovely, felted pumpkin Halloween decorations that can be made in a variety of colours.

You will need:

- Carded wool batts in shades of orange, yellow, brown and green
- Cocktail stick

1. Take a piece of your orange carded wool batt for your pumpkin, approximately 20cm x 13cm (8in x 5in), and place on your mat. Fold it in half lengthways, and then into three widthways, then roll it up tightly. Holding it firmly so it doesn't unroll, felt the ends down to hold it.

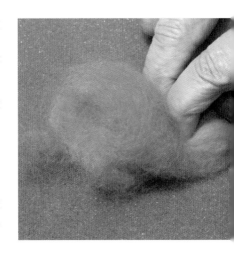

2. Holding your fingers on the top, felt all around the sides, gradually forming it into a rounded pumpkin shape. Turn it over so that you can felt the sides from both the top and bottom to get the

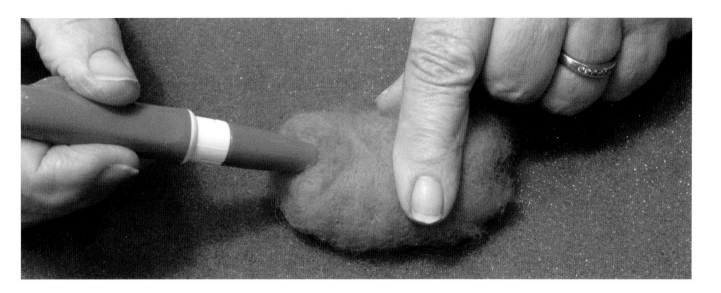

shape right. Felt until it is nicely round and firm, and then felt the top and bottom to firm these up as well.

3. Now add another layer of the same colour by wrapping it around the shape and felt until it is smooth.

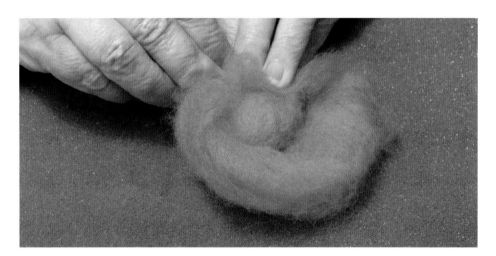

4. Now to add the markings on to the pumpkin; you can do this in brown or green. Take very thin wisps of wool, approximately 5cm (2in) long, and twist them between your fingers to make a thread. With a single 38 needle, start at the top of your pumpkin attaching the thread of wool, carefully stretching it out and felting it in, all the way down the sides to the middle of your pumpkin base. When you reach the bottom, snip off any excess wool with scissors. If you

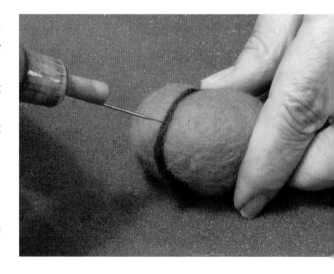

find your thread isn't long enough to reach the bottom, just make another thread and carry on where you left off. Once you have your line attached, felt it in firmly to create a slight indentation; if the brown wool disappears don't worry, just add another thread on the top so you are still able to see the lines. These will form the sections in the pumpkin. Add four lines to 'quarter' the pumpkin, then a line within each 'quarter', to give you eight sections. Don't worry at all if the sections are not all equal, as no pumpkin is perfectly shaped.

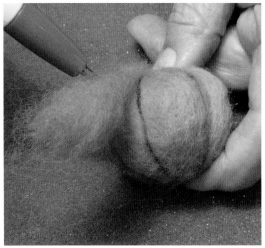

5. Now take small wisps of the pumpkin colour, ball them up in your fingers, and felt them in the sections between the lines to bulk them out. I tend to put more in the middle of the section, and not so much at the top or bottom, but you can make them as bulbous as you wish. You could add a wisp of a different shade or colour to your pumpkin while doing this.

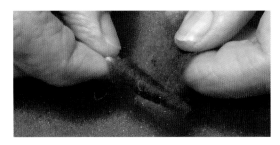

6. Now in either brown or green, make the stalk. Do this by wrapping a wisp of wool around a cocktail stick, to the thickness you want your stalk. Carefully, to avoid hitting the stick, felt it a few times while on the stick, then carefully remove it by pushing it off and needle felting it further until it is nice and firm, leaving it with a wispy end to attach it to the pumpkin. Once the stalk is well felted, attach this on the top of the pumpkin in the middle using a single needle to felt the wispy ends in.

7. Now take some green carded wool to make two (or more if you want) leaves. Pull off a small leaf-size wisp and felt it on your pad a little before folding it into a leaf shape and felting it until firm. Once they

are done, place the leaves on to the top of your pumpkin next to the stalk and use a single needle to felt these in until secure.

8. Now it is up to you what you do with your pumpkin! You could add some thin cord or thread to hang it up; you could add several on to a long cord to make a pumpkin garland; or, like the eggs, they look good with several pumpkins of different colours in a nice basket. You can make larger pumpkins in a variety of sizes by increasing the size of wool you start with; the amount of wool you add between the sections will also change them quite a bit.

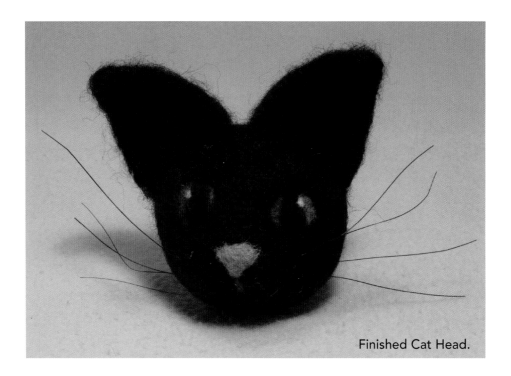

Finished Cat Head.

AUTUMN – HALLOWEEN WITCH'S BLACK CAT

A witch's black cat head that can be made into a brooch or decoration.

You will need:
- Black carded wool batt
- Coloured carded wool batts for the eyes
- Pink and white carded wool batt
- Whiskers
- Brooch back or magnet

1. Take a handful of black carded wool and fold the edges under to make an 8cm (3.5in) diameter circle. Lay it on your pad and, starting at the edges, felt diagonally towards the middle, working your way around the outside 2cm (1in) of the circle to get a firm edge, before felting the centre. Make sure you turn it over and felt the disc from both sides. The reason for doing the edge first is that if you felt the middle first, it pushes the wool outwards and you would end up with a large flat circle; doing it this way creates a formed and firm circle which holds the shape while you felt the centre. The aim here is to make this into a firmly felted disc of felt, around 5cm (2in) in diameter and 1cm (½in) in depth, so if it isn't quite large enough, you can wrap it with another layer of wool and felt it until it is firm and smooth.

2. Now you need to build up the face shape from a flat disc to a dome. To do this, take a wad of black carded wool (enough to form the dome on top), fold the edges under so it is slightly smaller than the disc, and then felt this on the top of the disc. Keeping it just in from the very edge, felt it all over until firm but not flat. If you don't have much of a dome, you need to repeat this step by adding wool in the middle until you have a dome shape. Once your dome is formed, take another thin layer of black wool and wrap it completely over the disc with the join at the back, and felt until smooth.

3. Take a single needle and felt two lines in the face, one down the middle and the other across the middle, to split the face into quarters, these are for markers so you don't need to needle felt these deep, just enough to see them; this will help keep the features level and in the correct place.

4. Now make two indentations for the eyes. Form these halfway between the side of the head and the centre, and just on or above the horizontal line, making them large enough to fit the tip of your index finger in.

5. I like to use green, orange or yellow for a witch's cat's eyes, and I also like to blend two colours together for them, but you can just use a single colour if preferred. To blend two colours, for example to make yellow eyes, take a small piece of yellow wool and a pinch of orange or gold, and stack them on top of each other. Then holding the wool at the ends, pull the stack apart and restack and repeat this until the colours are mixed up. Using a single needle, felt some of chosen eye colour wool into the indentations, putting in enough to fill them.

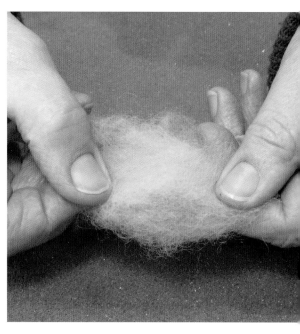

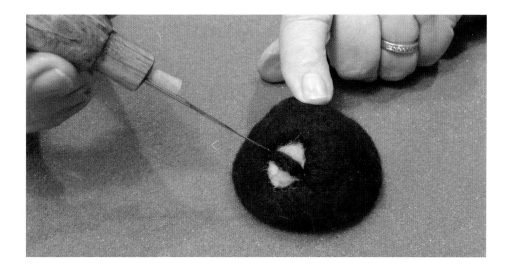

6. Take a tiny piece of black wool and fold into a small disc for the pupil and felt this into the centre of the eye. You can make the pupil whatever shape or size you like. Add a tiny dot of white in for light reflection by felting in. Repeat for the other eye.

7. Now take a piece of black wool, approximately 2cm x 2cm (1in x 1in), and fold the sides in, so it is just wide enough to sit between the eyes. Felt this on from the top of the head down between the eyes, smoothing it out at the bottom; this will form the bridge of the nose.

8. Take another piece of black wool, 5cm x 4cm (2in x 1.5in), fold it and felt this on widthways at the bottom of the nose for the muzzle area, reaching to and level with about halfway under the eyes. You could do this by adding two separate balls of wool if you find that works better for you.

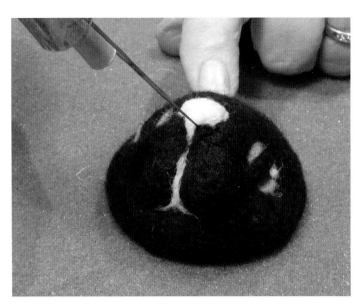

9. You can make the nose in a colour of your choice; I have done a black nose before, but it doesn't show up well on a black cat, so you could use a dull, dusty pink. Take a small piece of your chosen nose colour wool and fold it into a triangle and hold it on the face to check for size. Once happy, place this on the face with the point facing downwards and felt this on carefully with a single needle, starting around the edges first and then felt the middle as much as you need to smooth it. Now felt two tiny pieces of black wool either side of the bottom of the triangle for the nostrils. Then with another small piece of pink wool, twist it into a thread with your fingers and needle it in under the nose for his mouth.

10. Add some whiskers by threading them into the muzzle with a needle and adding a dab of glue to hold them in. I like to use black whiskers on a black cat, but use whatever colour you have.

11. The finished size of the head is approximately 5cm x 5cm (2in x 2in), so adjust your ear size accordingly if your project is smaller or larger. Take a piece of black wool and fold it into a triangle, the bottom edge being about half the width of the head; make two the same size. Add wisps of black wool if you can see any thin patches. Felt the ears on your pad with your punch or multi-needle tool, lifting occasionally so they don't get stuck. Carefully fold the very outside of the edges over and felt them down to give the ears a good defined edge. Leave the bottom edge curved and wispy for attaching them to the head.

12. Hold the ears against the head to check you are happy with the size. If satisfied, attach them using a single needle by firstly attaching the inside corner just slightly away from the centre of the head, felting it on just enough to hold it, and then curling the rest of the ear around the head and attaching the other corner to the side of the head. If you are unhappy with the position, carefully pull off and re-position. Once you are satisfied with the position, felt them on firmly and felt the rest of the ear in the middle into the head. Now add a wisp of black wool in both ears at the front and back to cover the join.

13. Now if you want to make this into a brooch, felt the back smooth and level, then sew or glue on the brooch back. You can then cover the bar with a piece of black wool, carefully felting either side of the bar.

Finished Snowman.

WINTER – CHRISTMAS SNOWMAN

Cute, winter snowmen decorations that can be made to any size you want.

You will need:

- Carded core wool batt
- White carded wool batt
- Black and orange carded wool batt
- Carded wool batt of various colours for hat, scarf and gloves
- Pipe cleaner
- Brown florist tape or brown carded wool batt
- Cocktail stick
- Glue
- Glitter card for base, or cord for hanging up

1. I usually make my mini snowmen approximately 9cm (3.5in) high, excluding the hat. To make a snowman this size, start by pulling off a piece of core wool and tease this into a piece approximately 20cm

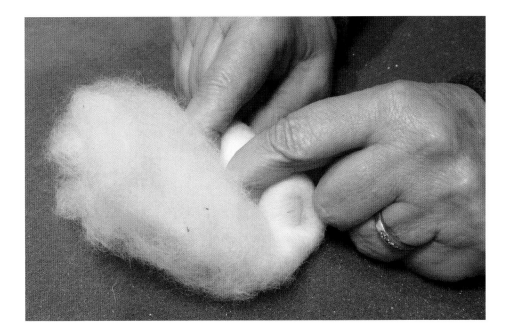

x 8cm (8in x 3in). Roll this up very tightly, folding the sides in as you go. Felt the ends down to hold it.

2. Now you need to get this sausage shape felted into an oval or a ball, depending on the shape you would like your snowman to be. Start by felting the ends towards the middle, this will start felting it down. Work on one end for a while and then turn it over and work from the other way, it should soon start to be more ball shaped. Once it is starting to form, you can squeeze the ball/oval in with your fingers from the ends while felting to help firm this up. Be careful doing this as it is easy to catch yourself with the needles; the safest way is to put the ball on the mat, squash it down with your fingers and felt it with the other hand. Your aim here is a nice firm ball or oval.

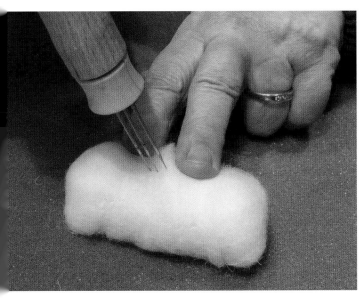

3. Usually, before I go on to using the white topcoat wool, I either get a new pad or simply turn my current one over to a clean side to avoid contaminating the white with any traces of other colours that may be stuck in the pad. Alternatively, you can get a piece of shop-bought wool felt in a light colour to lay on top of the pad.

4. Take a piece of white carded wool and tease into a circle large enough to cover the ball in one go. Wrap it around the ball, pull off any excess, and felt the white on to the ball/oval. Your body can be made round or oval so felt it accordingly as you go. To help keep it round, turn it constantly as you felt.

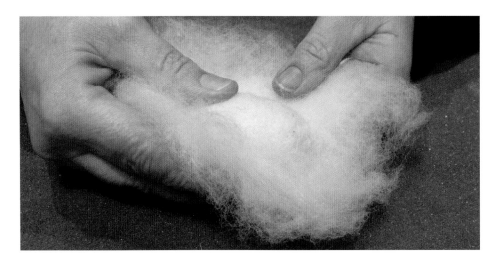

5. Now make a second ball for the head in the same way, but slightly smaller, to sit on top. If both balls end up a similar size, then just wrap another white layer around one of them and felt it on to make it larger until you can clearly see that one is bigger than the other.

6. Next join the two balls together. Do this by laying them on your pad, place a tiny wisp of white in the middle between the balls and then with a single 38 needle, felt them together holding them tightly together with your fingers. Work your way around the join felting from both directions, from one ball through into the other at the neck and felting the loose wool in between into both balls as well. Keep felting them until they are holding together nice and firmly.

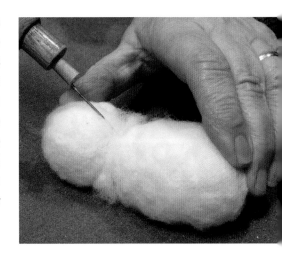

7. I now like to build the face area up a bit before adding the features, so that it doesn't look flat, but if you prefer a flatter face, you can move straight on to the next step. To add to the face, take a small piece of white wool and fold it into a flat rectangle, then felt this across the middle of the face to build up the area where the mouth, chin and nose will go. Then add two small balls either side for chubby cheeks. Then cover all this with a thin wisp of white to cover any joins you may have. Felt it on lightly with fine needles and make sure to felt around the cheeks to keep them prominent.

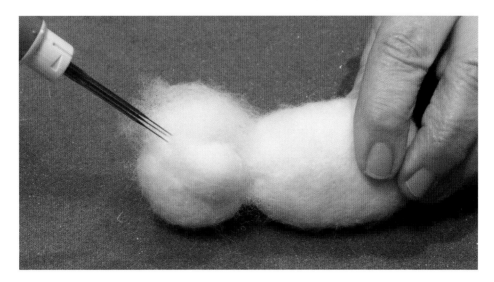

8. Next add the nose. I like making a traditional, carrot nose. To do this, take a very small wisp of orange, and wrap it around the very tip of a cocktail stick, making sure to keep the wool on the end with your fingers, and don't let it travel down the stick or you will end

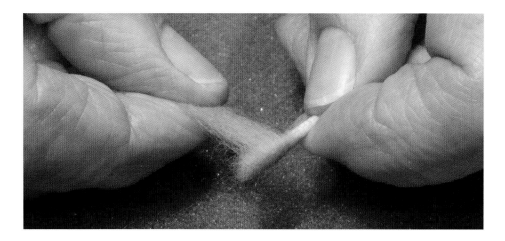

up with a very long nose. Carefully pull it off the stick and felt it just a few times so that it holds together, leaving some wispy ends for joining it to the face. Felt the point in a little bit to keep it in place. Now attach it to the face, holding it between the cheeks, and felt around the outside of the nose only, attaching it firmly. You can add a simple round orange ball if you prefer; just take a piece of orange, bobble it up in your fingers and felt it on.

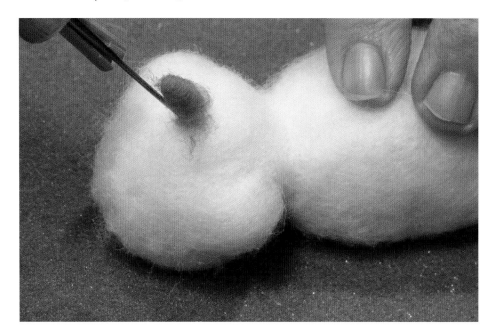

9. Now you can add a smiley mouth with some black wool. Take a tiny wisp of wool and roll it between your fingers to make a thread. Lay this on the face where you want your mouth to be, usually sitting between the cheeks, and with a single needle attach it one end, lay it along the face and felt it in, in the length and shape you require, pulling or trimming off any excess. Your preferences will come to you through practising; you can always make a spare ball just to practise on if you wanted to! Attach the features lightly first so you can just take them off if you don't like them and try again.

10. Now to add the eyes using black wool. Pull off a tiny wisp of wool, tease into a small circle or line and felt on to the face.

11. Once your features are on and you are happy, you can build up the cheeks a little more if you wish, but just add a very small amount of wool at a time. I like to add a little bit of pastel chalk to the cheeks as well, or you can use some face blush or a felt pen (but practise that first as you won't be able to remove it.)

12. Now the face is done, decide if you want the body to be a little plumper, I usually end up adding a little more now. To do this just wrap the body with another layer and felt it in. It looks better if the bottom half is a bit larger than the head.

13. Next give him a hat! You can do a hat in a variety of different styles. I will show you the hat used on this snowman, then you can have a go at other styles once you have made a few and got the idea. Decide on the colour of batting and lay out a triangle of it on your pad. The bottom edge needs to be wide enough to go all the way around the head, with about 2.5cm (1in) extra to allow for overlapping to join the sides together. The height of the triangle will determine the length of the hat so if you want a hat that is long enough to bend over at the top you need to allow for this in the height. If you have a punch tool then now is the perfect time to use it, as you want to needle felt this into a piece of flat felt which will then wrap around the head to form the hat, but any multi-needle

tool will do. Felt the triangle all over, leaving one edge a little wispy for joining it together – do felt that edge but just not as solidly as the rest. Fold the bottom of the triangle up and felt a small hem so that you get a tidy edge. Make sure you lift the piece regularly and turn it over so that you felt it from both sides. Add any pattern you want, such as dots or stripes, and felt it firmly with your Clover punch tool. Wrap the triangle around the head and check it all fits before attaching it. You can stretch it a bit with a tug if it isn't quite meeting. Holding the front of the hat at the level you want it to sit above the eyes, felt it a few times to hold it in place and then turn over to the back and join the edges. Felt these together on to the head. Now, with it laying on your pad, felt the wispy edges together all the way up to the top of the hat by felting it crossways. You can leave the top of the hat standing up or you can fold it down by folding and attaching the end to the body. You can add a little bobble by lightly felting a small ball and then felting the top point

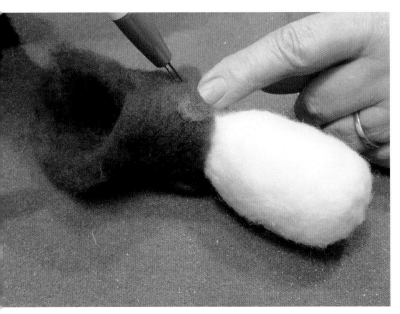

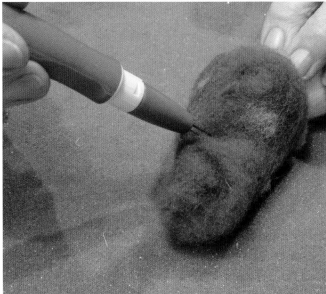

of the hat into it to attach it, or you could stitch it on. You could also add a little metal bell if you prefer.

14. Make a scarf by taking a long thin strip of batting and fold it into two or three depending on the width you have at the neck. Felt this until firm with your punch tool. It needs to be long enough to go around the neck at least once, to tie up and for it to hang down as well so allow for this in the length. You can tie this on and leave it like that, or you can tie it and then felt it lightly in certain places to fix it on.

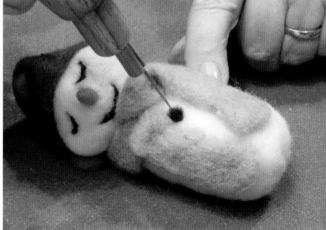

15. You can needle felt buttons on down the front by taking tiny wisps of black or your choice of colour wool, rolling them in your fingers and felting them on.

16. You could also add arms and gloves. Cut your pipe cleaner to the length you want your arms, allowing at least an extra 1cm (½in) to glue into the body, so somewhere around 5–7cm (2–3in). Cover

the pipe cleaner with your brown florist tape or brown wool. The tape should stick itself, but if required add a little glue to secure this at the ends. If using brown wool, take a thin strip and wrap it around the pipe cleaner by turning the pipe cleaner with one hand, holding the wool on the pipe cleaner tightly with your finger and thumb on the opposite hand. Choose a colour of carded batt for your gloves and taking a small strip, wrap it around the very end of the arm and felt it flat. With an awl, make a hole into the sides of the snowman; you need to get the thicker end of the awl into the snowman to make a large enough hole. Leave the awl in place while you pop some glue on the end of the arm and then remove the awl and as quickly as you can push the arm into the hole, as it can close up fairly swiftly! Needle a little white wool into the hole around the arm; this will help hold it in place while the glue dries. Repeat with the other arm.

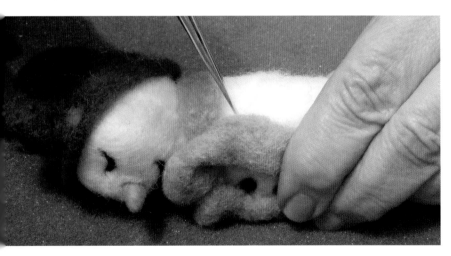 

17. You can attach your snowman onto a piece of ribbon or thread to make it into a hanging decoration. However, I like to make this a standing decoration. To do this, cut a circle out of glitter card for your base. Use your punch tool or multi tool to flatten the snowman's bottom, then put a big blob of glue on the snowman's bottom and stick it on to your card, holding it there for a minute or two, or propping it up, until it dries. It looks very sweet if you have a group of them all with different hats and scarves.

Owl and penguin.

WINTER – CHRISTMAS PENGUINS AND OWLS

Fun, Christmas decorations, both made with the same base shape.

You will need:
- Black and white carded wool batt for the penguins
- Brown or grey and white carded wool batt for the owls
- Orange and yellow carded wool batt for the beaks
- Various wool batt colours for hats
- Acrylic 14mm owl eyes
- Cocktail stick
- Cord for hanging them

1. In this section, you will make a basic shape from core wool and then turn it into either a penguin or owl by simply changing the colours you use. Take a piece of core wool, approximately 15cm x 8cm (6in x 3in), roll it up lengthways as tightly as you can, folding the sides into the middle as you roll.

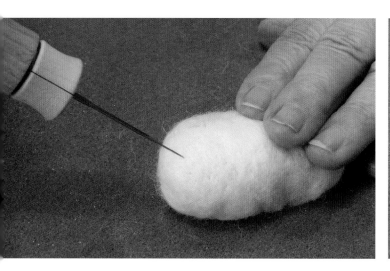

2. Felt down the join and then start to needle felt it all over, turning it as you go and felting the ends of the shape as well; you are wanting to make the ends rounded, so felt accordingly to shape it into an oval. Once done, cover the oval in the colour appropriate for the body colour of the bird you are making. I have done white for the penguin and grey for the owl here.

3. You are aiming for this to be approximately 7cm (2.5in) tall and 4cm (1.5in) wide. If yours is a little small, add more wool in layers and felt them on firmly until your piece is the desired size.

4. Now this is where you add the different colours to make your project either an owl or a penguin. Here, I have done the penguin, but for the owl version just change the colour to whatever you want it to be.

5. Now you need to lightly felt a piece of wool in the coat colour (black for the penguin, colour of choice for the owl). Lay a solid but thin layer out on your pad, large enough to cover the back, the top of the head and part of the sides. Lay the body on this to give you a rough guide, but don't worry too much as you can patch areas later if you need to.

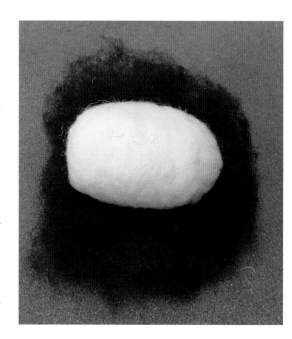

6. Felt the wool on your pad with your punch or multi tool, enough to just start it felting before adding it to the body, you don't need to needle felt it too much as you will felt it more once it is on your penguin.

7. Now felt it firmly on to the body, leaving the sides a little loose ready to shape into the wings, and folding all the other edges in as you attach them to get a neat line.

8. Now to shape the wings. Using the loose wool at the sides, fold the edges in and felt so that it is neat, you can finish the wing at the sides or as far round the tummy as you want, perhaps curling around the body slightly, meeting in the middle, or you can put them slightly apart or one above the other.

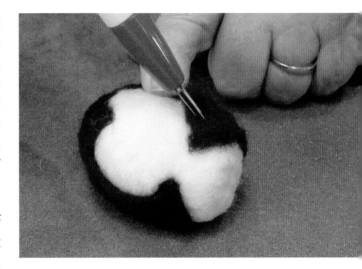

9. Check over the body now and if there are any areas on the coat that are not quite covered, or look thin, cover them with wisps of matching wool.

10. On the top of the head, you need to form a point over the eye area. You may have enough wool there already to do this but if not, take a small piece of matching wool, fold it into a pointed triangle and felt this on.

11. You should have a good amount of white on here to allow for the eye area, but this will depend a little on how wide the point on the top of the head is. If you need to, take some

white wool, fold it into a small circle and felt it on to the eye area, making sure not to cover the point up.

12. Now for the penguin, felt in two tiny wisps of black for the eyes, leaving space between for the beak, and not placing these too high, as you don't want to cover them with the hat later. Add a tiny spot of white in the eyes if you want to. Another option for penguin eyes is to use black glass or acrylic eyes by creating holes using an awl and glueing the eyes in. For an owl, you can use brown and yellow wool for the eyes, or you can use plastic eyes as used in the owl chapter. I also like to add a line of a darker colour around a glass eye.

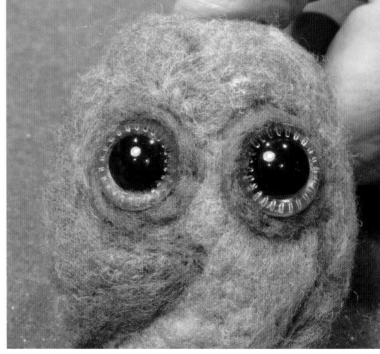

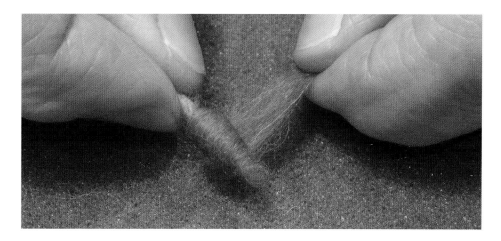

13. Still with the penguin … to make the beak, take a small wisp of orange or yellow wool and wrap it around the point of a cocktail stick. Hold your fingers on the wool and twizzle the stick a few times; this will help hold the wool together as the warmth of your fingers will felt it a bit. If making an owl beak, this needs to be slightly larger than the penguin. Remove the beak from the stick and with a very fine needle, gauge 40 or 42, felt it all over and make sure the point is firm. Now attach the beak to the face by felting the loose wool at the wide end into the face, between the eyes. For the penguin, I usually leave the beak pointing out, just felting it in as much as you need to hold it on firmly. For an owl, you can attach the beak in the same way, then fold it down and attach it at the bottom as well.

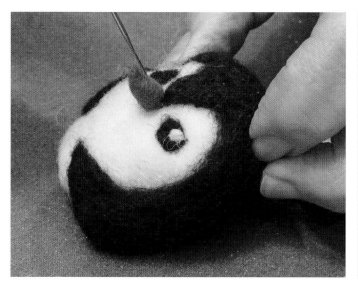

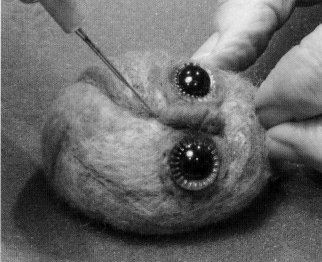

14. Check all over your work to see if anywhere needs building up, or any edges need tidying. Add wisps of wool to build up, or felt down areas that need tidying.

15. If you would prefer a fluffy finish to your penguin or owl, add

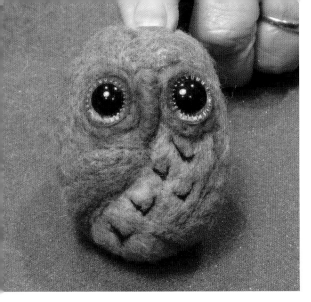

a thin wispy layer of wool all over and only lightly felt it on.

16. I usually make the owl slightly larger than the penguin, so you just start the process with a larger piece of core wool. You can add owl markings on its chest with tiny pieces of wool, either dots or small V shapes, by taking tiny wisps and felting these on.

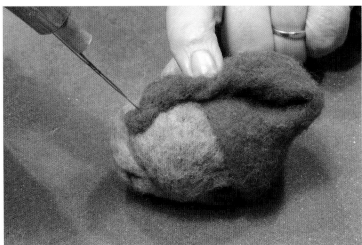

17. Now you can make a Santa hat in the same way as you did the snowman hat (refer back to the snowman section for the method if you need to). Make the triangle, attach it to the head in the same way, then laying the hat on the pad, felt the edges together across the join, fold it over and attach to the body with the bobble. To make a simple bobble hat without the long point,

make your triangle shorter. Once attached to the head, felt the top down towards the head, make it look neat and then add the bobble.

18. Finally, add some thread to make this into a hanging decoration. Or felt the bottom nice and flat to make a standing decoration; you can glue him on to a wood slice or piece of sturdy card if you want to have him standing.

Bunny Heads.

Easter Egg Bowl.

Pumpkin Stack.

2 Penguins with Hats.

Group of Snowmen.

2 Witches Black Cats.

Stockists

Adelaide Walker	**www.adelaidewalker.co.uk**
Heidifeathers	**www.heidifeathers.com**
Living Felt	**www.feltingsupplies.livingfelt.com**
The Felt Box	**www.thefeltbox.co.uk**
The Makerss	**www.themakerss.co.uk**
World of Wool	**www.worldofwool.co.uk**

Acknowledgements

I would like to thank all my family and friends for their support and encouragement in making this book. There are a few individuals I would like to personally thank for specific help.

Firstly, Marie Spaulding from Living Felt, for her permission to use her own Wooly Wednesday Owl tutorial to create my own owl in Chapter 3.

Next, I would like to thank my children, Edgina and Oliver for their help and patience, my daughter Scarlett for her help with editing and producing the book.

Finally, I would like to thank my husband, Mark; brother-in-law, Nick Rees; and sister, Christine Rees; for all their help with the photography throughout the book.